MAKING D

MAKING DIFFICULTIES
RESEARCH AND THE CONSTRUCTION OF SPECIAL EDUCATIONAL NEEDS

Edited by
Peter Clough and Len Barton

P·C·P
Paul Chapman
Publishing Ltd

Chapter 1 and Chapter 10
Copyright © 1995, Peter Clough and Len Barton.
All other material © 1995 Paul Chapman Publishing.

Paul Chapman Publishing Ltd
144 Liverpool Road
London
N1 1LA

British Library Cataloguing in Publication Data

Making Difficulties: Research and the
Construction of Special Educational Needs
I. Clough, Peter   II. Barton, Len
371.9

ISBN 1 85396 294 5

Typeset by Whitelaw & Palmer Ltd, Glasgow
Printed and bound by
Athenaeum Press Ltd, Gateshead, Tyne & Wear.

A B C D E F G H   9 8 7 6 5

CONTENTS

1

INTRODUCTION:
SELF AND THE RESEARCH ACT

Peter Clough and Len Barton

How we as researchers view disability will be crucial in relation to how we interact with disabled people in our research projects. The extent to which through experience we develop alternative perspectives, and/or revise existing understandings, needs to be carefully monitored. Thus, it is essential that we critically engage with our presuppositions and challenge disabilist assumptions. This is not a simple or once-and-for-all activity; rather it is a process which we need continually and seriously to pursue. The outcome of such a learning experience will influence, for example, how, when and why we involve disabled people in our research projects. This includes the points of planning and not merely the stages of implementation. From this perspective, as Barton (1988, p. 91) advocates,

> Research is not a value neutral activity. It is a social experience in which the subjects of research can suffer and perceive particular forms of study as oppressive. This raises a further issue: to what extent are researchers, including teachers-as-researchers, prepared to put their skills and knowledge at the service of the researched? This includes involving them in discussions about the choice of a topic of investigation, as well as the possible use to which findings or insights are put.

Disabled researchers are critical of the existing conditions of research production. The social relations involved support a strong distinction between the researcher and the researched. The former have the necessary significant knowledge and skills. It is they who therefore need to control the research agenda and process (Abberley, 1992; Barnes, 1992; Oliver, 1992). Much of the research has been strongly influenced by positivist assumptions. This has legitimated a form of psychological and individual reductionism which views

'. . . . the problem which disabled people face as being caused by their own impairments' (Oliver, 1992, p. 108). Within this tradition there exists a powerful ideological role given to the discourse of objectivity (Zarb, 1992). The position of funding bodies and policy-makers in supporting these relations of research production have been important.

These particular concerns are significant in relation to the field of study the contributions in this volume are exploring. The subjects of study experience institutional discrimination and their voice is essentially excluded from educational discourse. The changing definitions of difference which shape their lives and opportunities are not '. . . the expression of a group of people finding their own identity, their own history' (Ryan and Thomas, 1990, p. 13). They are the recipients of powerful professional categories. These envelope their identities. They are the 'lunatics', the 'idiots', the 'mentally handicapped', the 'subnormal', the 'spastics', the 'cripples' and 'level-one child'. The point is: *We* know who *They* are. They are conspicuous, because their world is set about with a particularly forceful categorical thinking. The extent to which researchers take on the mantle of these generalized social, public constructions is a serious issue. It is impossible to work in this field without being in some way conditioned by this categorical hegemony. They are identified by what they cannot do, what is wrong with them. Difference, essentially viewed in negative terms, lies deep at the heart of this discourse. In this context 'normality' is a tyrannical means by which these individuals are socialized into 'learnt helplessness' and a culture of dependency.

This book therefore calls for, and demonstrates, ways of working which are critical, self-conscious and change oriented. The accounts presented attempt to problematize subject, object and method as different moments of the same process in experience. The principal aim of this book is to provide insight into the ways in which, for example, 'special educational need' is variously constructed through research. The book therefore attempts to show the mutual construction of content and method in the creation of a wide range of topics. In particular, contributions seek to convey the crucial *experience* of research. We proceed from the view that 'Special Educational Need' is variously constructed in the social interactions which characterize this field of study. However, the very assumption that there is such a 'field', and – what is more – that is some way 'given', obscures the processes by which knowledge is generated and validated and thus fails to problematize the very terms and issues which research purports to address.

The book reasserts the view that research does not merely address or discover the objects of its inquiry, but that it begins to create them from the first moment of identification of a topic; *how* we choose to research a subject is itself constitutive of that subject. In this respect, to select a 'method' is to attach immediately a quite particular view and a particular ideology. While these views may hold for all research in the social sciences, they seem particularly poignant in this sphere of inquiry, a field known – at least to practitioners

– by the routine collision of judgement and value with power and interest.

In a sense this collection attempts to go slightly further 'behind the scenes' than is usually involved in the description of research processes. This involves examining issues relating to self and the research act. Thus a key interest is in the ways in which the personal construction of phenomena contribute to the social and hence institutionalized nature of the field. For (as we have argued above) research itself creates – rather than merely studies – the phenomenon of special education/disability, and hence the constructs which researchers themselves bring to the work are important determinants not only of the success of the study itself but indeed also of the nature and direction of the field itself.

A great deal of published research takes its terms for granted, usually by attaching 'methods' which in the research community we understand as self-justifying. What we hope to have achieved in this book, however, is a much more fundamental problematizing of the areas under study by asking our authors to confront questions such as the following:

- What assumptions about SEN/disability do I have which are inevitably present in the way I conceive of the study?
- What specific questions – in the light of these – am I asking in this particular study, and which events and circumstances prompted them and gave them a particular urgency?
- Why and how did these assumptions, questions and circumstances suggest or require the particular methods which I chose? What assumptions about 'how the world operates' – and how we can know it – are given with these methods? Why, then, are they particularly suitable for investigating the phenomena in question?
- How did the process of my research change or qualify my assumptions? In what ways am I changed by the research?
- And in what ways is the community's understanding changed by what I have achieved? If, as we are trying to suggest, research actually defines the field, what redefinition (however small) is suggested in my work? What might – or what would I have – another researcher learn from my experience?

Each author has attempted to address some of these questions, and what they have sought to achieve is a self-critical approach to this research.

What is evident from an examination of a range of research conducted in this area is the tendency on the part of some researchers to identify a 'good' or 'sound' study in terms of its failure to disclose the presence of the author. In these cases it is customary to show how clean were the instruments used by arguing their distinctness from us as persons. These are tools, no more; but also no less; and as such we know they were made by other people to such and such a specification for this and that job. We can measure the research by knowing which tools were used.

The biggest lie that a so-called 'methodology' tells is of the distance between us and our work; hence we elaborate the clinical nature, the sterile cleanliness of the instruments we use. When researchers attach this or that method, they place filters between their perceptions and the objects under study. In the social sciences, methods are readily to hand: the interview, the survey questionnaire, the structured observation – all these and more mediate between what the researcher sees and what the object is for itself. But what we want to say is, *the forms of these inquiries make for the form of the object as it is finally realized in the research report*. Research changes objects; it constitutes objects as what a research form requires them to be.

We do not underestimate the difficulties involved in moving to the sorts of research practices we have briefly identified in these opening comments. Indeed, Shotter (1993, p. 48) captures most powerfully some of the key dimensions involved when he criticizes various research positions:

> By our insistence upon the use of certain 'professional' textual practices, we do not allow ourselves to be influenced in our identities, as the academic professionals we are. Thus, no matter how benevolent we may be towards those we study – no matter how concerned with 'their' liberation, with their betterment, with preventing 'their' victimisation, etc. – the fact is that 'we' do not make sense of 'their' lives in 'their' terms. 'We' *do not even* make sense of 'their' lives 'with them'. While what they say is treated as 'data', they themselves are not treated seriously as being able to speak the truth about their own lives; their claims do not pass 'our' institutional tests.

Although these criticisms have a general applicability with regard to research mentalities and practices, they have particular significance in relation to the subjects of the research accounts in this book. They experience, in different degrees of intensity, ideological, material and social oppression, powerfully expressed through institutional discrimination and forms of exclusion which support a less-than-human categorization.

Critical reflection on the relationship between self and the research process involves exploring and exposing the hidden and taken-for-granted aspects of the social relations of research production. Reflective self-awareness over the methods, commitments, excitements, anger and mistakes of the research act are elements of this task. This is necessary because, as Clough says (p. 138) 'we ourselves do not come innocent to a research task, or a situation of events; rather, we situate these events not merely in the institutional meaning which our profession provides but also constitute them as expressions of ourselves'.

CONCLUSION

Given the motivation behind the production of this collection of accounts it is vitally important that we ask our readers: can we, should we and do we need to know what researchers are thinking behind the accounts they choose to show us in their professional writing? This collection is based on the view that what we as researchers think and, importantly, where we are coming from, inevitably influences how we construct things.

If, as we are claiming, the values of the researcher are indispensably present in the conception and realization of a project, then this presence should not only be discernible without doing damage to the validity of the research but should indeed also enhance the claim of the work to make morally and politically important statements. This includes the extent to which the participants found the experience of the research process to be challenging and enabling.

REFERENCES

Abberley, P. (1992) 'Counting us out: a discussion of the OPCS disability surveys', *Disability, Handicap and Society*, Vol. 7, no. 2, pp. 139–56 (special issue).

Barnes, C. (1992) 'Qualitative research: valuable or irrelevant', *Disability, Handicap and Society*, Vol. 7, no. 2, pp. 115–24 (special issue).

Barton, L. (1988) 'Research and practice: the need for alternative perspectives', in L. Barton (ed.) *The Politics of Special Educational Need*. Falmer Press, Lewes.

Oliver, M. (1992) 'Changing the social relations of research production?', *Disability, Handicap and Society*, Vol. 7, no. 2, pp. 101–14 (special issue).

Ryan, J. and Thomas, F. (1990) *The Politics of Mental Handicap*. Penguin Books, Harmondsworth.

Shotter, J. (1993) *Cultural Politics of Everyday Life*. Open University Press, Buckingham.

Zarb, G. (1992) 'On the road to Damascus: first steps towards changing the relations of disability research production', *Disability, Handicap and Society*, Vol. 7, no. 2, pp. 125–38 (special issue).

2

EXCOMMUNICATING THE SEVERELY DISABLED:[1] STRUGGLES, POLICY AND RESEARCHING

Gillian Fulcher

The role of the intellectual is to be a dissident: he [*sic*] should not speak for his class, or group or race.

(Alain Touraine, in Melbourne, 8 July 1993)

What is important as the starting point of analysis depends on its objectives; it is not given in the essential structure of society. Insofar as those objectives are political, the way social relations are analysed will be informed by political concerns and objectives.

(Hindess, 1986, p. 115)

In August 1991 the phone rang. Was I interested in undertaking a research project in the general area of severe disability, communication and government policy which, specifically, might address the frustrations of recreation workers in non-government agencies who were expected to implement government policy? I'd not met the caller: a senior lecturer in recreation studies at one of Melbourne's many tertiary institutions. I was immediately interested. He had limited monies. At the rate that had recently been established by federal government policy for researchers with specific qualifications, this allowed a ten-week half-time project. These were almost laughable conditions for such a complex project that would need to speak to diverse audiences. Nevertheless, we negotiated arrangements very easily (a fractional, part-time appointment at the institution), and the very positive condition which made the project possible was the total freedom I had to carry out the work as I might best conceive it. In an age of regulomania (outcomes, objectives, methods: write it all down and we will monitor you – oh yes, and there will be these meetings with the Steering Committee) this was unusual.[2] In the event, the project took another three weeks half-time longer than the appointment.

WHY DO IT?

I was highly interested in the topic, having researched, in a number of capacities, disability issues and policy, either full time or as part of an academic role, since 1981. The most formative of these experiences had been my work as main writer and researcher and policy analyst for a Ministerial Review of Educational Services for the Disabled; this involved a year's secondment from 1983 to 1984 to the then Department of Education and Science and it provided a range of experiences, insights and problematics which have remained with me since. The policy struggles with which I engaged in the review are, by a series of separate practices, direct antecedents of the policy struggles I was to take on in this project in 1991. To spell out their connections, a brief historical excursion is necessary, though it will have to collapse a more interesting tale into simplicities.

A HISTORICAL NOTE

In 1982, when the Victorian Ministerial Review of Educational Services for the Disabled began its work, the Warnock Report, *Special Educational Needs* (1978), was highly regarded by some members of the review, such that members of the Warnock Committee had visited the Education Department, talked with various members of the review and met with its chair. When I entered the review's meetings, in February 1983, I brought a sociological view of categories and their often unfortunate consequences, drawing, in this particular area, on Sally Tomlinson's (1982) book *A Sociology of Special Education*, just published. It seemed clear, as events have borne out, that the idea of special educational needs was a new category, a master status that would perform exactly the same functions as earlier disability-related categories, and that it was a euphemism for failure (Barton, 1986). Hence, in this policy arena, in the acts of meeting with and writing for the review, I struggled against the idea of special educational needs, and a key principle in the report became that of non-categorization: an idea which many found difficult to understand and which was the topic of prolonged struggles in and outside the review's meetings or arenas. Nowhere in the report of the review does the term special educational needs appear: a struggle thus won *at that stage*, in that particular arena. With hindsight it is easy to see that the idea of non-categorization seeks to avoid the dilemmas which Barton and Tomlinson (1981) (Tomlinson, 1982) have shown characterize this area, and that such avoidance sets up other dilemmas. This is to raise discussions in political theory outside the present discussion, and beyond the cognizance it would seem of any who sat around the review's table at that time. In addition to the idea of non-categorization (a principle for practice: how these ideas worry me now), I proposed the idea of problems in schooling to signify, somewhat clumsily, an overnight conceptualization, the understanding that schools may handicap students.

Since 1984 policy has been remade (as it always may be, and as I found, in my later researching (Fulcher, 1989; 1993), seeking to understand more broadly the struggles in which I had been engaged) so that, in 1992, not only is the idea of special educational needs well established in Victoria but even the idea of 'critical needs' is part of official discourse (General Manager, Southern Metropolitan Region, 1990). Some suggest the idea of critical needs has replaced the notion of problems in schooling.

While the 1984 report did not include the idea of special educational needs, nor even that of needs, it contributed, by its prominence in debates in educational and related policy arenas, to a discourse on needs, whose sources are of course much wider. Thus in recreation policy for disabled people in 1991, the idea of needs appeared and, as in other policy areas, the idea of actors freely choosing their action: the idea of 'choice', a long-standing concern in liberal philosophy. It is through these contending discourses and these policy struggles – those in which I and others engaged in the review in 1983 and 1984, and I in the 1991 project – that these arenas are, by a series of indirect practices (much in the way that Miller and Rose, 1990, outline), directly related. It was thus in a different arena but *in the same struggle* that I engaged with policy in 1991. The terms in policy may shift but the *struggles remain*.

In the 1991 project, the ideas in recreation policy for disabled people newly render the categories of the 1980s. Thus at the centre of the 1991 project lay a discourse and a spectre: the figure of a severely disabled person, typically in a wheelchair, without 'speech', generally with severe cerebral palsy, and seen as 'deficient' but as deserving the same rights as other Australians (Hindess, 1991a) allegedly enjoy. The audiences for the report I was to write in 1992 might differ in their views of policy, in their immediate concerns, and in their positions or particular responsibilities but they shared, I suspected, this spectre: though the senior lecturer's brief carefully avoided the construction of a person deficient and 'unable to communicate'. It was this spectre – and its centrality – which I had to remove: this was a key to different policy practices: declaring the deficit model was technically wrong and morally undesirable, and that it derived from structural oppression of the severely disabled person and of others would be of limited value. It would, more likely, lose each of the audiences. Here, as in my research for *Disabling Policies?*, I took the stance Barry Hindess advises: '. . . the way social relations are analysed will be informed by political concerns and objectives' (Hindess, 1986, p. 115), adding to it, as his work implies, a clear distinction between policy analysis and political theorizing.

THE POLICY STRUGGLE

It was against these ideas – a discourse about the severely disabled and a spectre – that I would now engage. But is this to move beyond the topic of special educational needs? No: the idea of special educational needs is one instance of a range of categories which oppress disabled people. Furthermore, the categories of thought which inhabit government-level discourse, policy areas and arenas, and which structure vocational academic concerns, are themselves part of the problem: we have to shift these apparent boundaries, look behind the specificity of terms, if we are to analyse usefully: to understand the broad practices which underlie the constitution of what, at the everyday level, we see as separate. Moreover, the terms are essentially shifting. Bourdieu, in *The Logic of Practice* (1990, p. 141), summarizes both this shifting and the struggle:

> The specific efficacy of subversive action consists in the power to bring to consciousness, and so modify, the categories of thought which help to orient individual and collective practices and in particular the categories through which distributions are perceived and appreciated . . . Each state of the social world is thus no more than a temporary equilibrium . . . The struggle . . . is . . . a struggle to appropriate rare goods and a struggle to impose the legitimate way of perceiving the power relations manifested by the distributions, a representation which, through its own efficacy, can help to perpetuate or subvert these power relations.

My central struggle with policy then was this: if knowledge is constitutive of power, as Foucault has argued, and if welfare and social policy are constitutive of both power and 'the social' (as Hewitt, 1983, argues of Foucault's account), then research, which seeks to provide knowledge in policy areas, its nature, is crucial. The struggle in research, as a series of practices which produce 'knowledge', becomes that of attempting to offer knowledge which is, for the moment, useful to the oppressed or less powerful, whoever they are: in this case, not only severely disabled people but surely also recreation workers, accountable to their consciences and their agency managers, public servants accountable to their ministers, and a researcher on a fractional appointment who might attempt such offerings?

A critical question was: How could I research this topic without further entrenching the 'object' of the research? I saw the taken-for-granted object as the severely disabled person, seen as deficient, viewed as having, and required by some simplistic slogan, to exercise 'choice' in his or her recreation. My aim was to replace this object with another, to reconstitute the topic and its central figure so that at the centre was government policy, the nature of policy and of politics. My awareness of the contribution of categories is not only intellectual, not only an intellectual problem when I write or research in the area of disability and say, education (as I specifically attempted to argue, for instance, in 1990b) but also a personally painful experience in everyday life: containing utterances – being inhibited – which others are free to mouth.

PRACTICALITIES AND THEIR CONCEPTUALIZATIONS, OR 'METHOD'

The project was broad. However, did I think it might be possible to grapple with such a complex task in so short a time? What methods would I use? The brief required me to

> . . . identify the nature of communication difficulties experienced by people with severe disabilities and strategies developed for dealing with this by relevant professions; review ethical questions related to decision making on behalf of non-communicating people; review disability policy and identify goals relevant to recreation for people with severe disabilities, in particular, goals relevant to questions of communication; develop program principles on which practice methodologies can be developed.
>
> (Duty Statement, Project Stage 1)

The topic of recreation programmes . . . ? We used to call these things activities or leisure before technobabble[3] took over. Sometimes I find it useful to think of earlier authors whose vocabulary is wider: it helps broaden and liberate my understanding. Will a new Keats write of nightingales now that bird calls are reduced to 'information'?[4] A wider vocabulary helps create that distance, so necessary for critique,[5] between the researcher and the topic: a tenuous, momentary distance, yes, but one which has to be held so as to make that momentary offering. I shall try again . . .

The topic of recreation programmes for severely disabled people raises linguistic, neurophysiological, cultural, political, philosophical and moral matters: all are complex, controversial and enter wide-ranging debate. This last phrase I've copied from the report and you may notice the writing style has suddenly changed: from discursive to terse: so much to be said: how to say it all within a manageable report where I would be doing not only the gathering, defining, conceptualizing and sifting, of what we call the research material but also much of the wordprocessing?

The audiences for the report were diverse: recreation workers in non-government agencies, mainly young and female, policy people in the Department of Sport and Recreation, a senior lecturer in recreation studies, students in those courses. Each became an audience for each, in my view, are engaged with policy, not as a matter of 'implementation', for this is to misread, mistake the nature of policy practices, but because policy is made at all levels (Hindess, 1986; Fulcher, 1986; 1989, among others).

Each audience had different concerns: the recreation workers with their consciences, with being accountable to their managers, and with reducing the frustrations in their work (I may have taken him to the zoo or the beach for the day, and have helped lug his wheelchair into the society's van but he can't speak and I don't know if he's had a good day, whether that was his choice or whether I've met his special needs). The public servants' concerns were with funding programmes in metropolitan and country Victoria, with 'implementing', 'integration' policy as they saw this, with the principles for these programmes, with their outcomes and with being accountable to people higher in the department's hierarchy and to the minister. Each audience, I assumed, brought differing though, at times, shared views on the topics I was to cover. I sought to discover the nature of these frameworks: these frameworks were a central part of the research material I would gather.

How to reach such a diverse audience? This is the quintessential teaching problem: that of an audience with different backgrounds, concerns and starting points: notice I saw the task as one of teaching not quasi-politicking: what I wrote would be political as in all social science. There would be analysis with political implications but it would not be tempered as rhetoric, nor as measured critique, to appease the powerful. Laurel Richardson's (1990) *Writing Strategies* appealed not only because it addressed the problem of reaching different audiences but also because it put writing in its political context. ('Writing is, thus, not opposed to practice but is a political practice'; Richardson, 1990, p. 64, drawing on Lather, 1988). Her ideas provided a tactic: I would write differently in different parts of the report, to appeal to different audiences; at the same time, the content and style must carry along the other audiences, it must engage them too. And brevity was so clearly necessary – or it would take too long to say – and this too would lose the audiences, or so I am told. Clearly I conceived the task as one of creating self-reflexivity in the reader.

Time and the need for brevity were not the only constraints. Controversy was another: it was a major characteristic of the material and the context in which I would have to work. The struggles for authority and legitimacy surrounding communication and severely disabled people in Victoria are intense, known internationally for these, by definition, unresolved debates. I would also have to cover hugely complex technical material (in neurophysiological and other processes). A glossary I decided, at some stage, would help. But not your ordinary definitive glossary. It would oppose definitions: expose the contrasts between these and their frameworks. This would show the technicalities and their limits.

So I posed these questions to myself – in working out what we call the research design. A gender analysis would not help nor would an openly partisan view of the disabled person as oppressed: neither would achieve my objective. I hoped, I suppose, as I reached to find my own assumptions, that I could lead to a different reason based, in part, on a different understanding of the politics – the role of the political – in all of this. I saw that the task was not merely that of showing how the idea of special needs is an idea, not a positive fact about people, nor that it is sometimes a politically dangerous position for disability groups and disabled people to adopt in politics – and that challenging that is a dangerous position for a researcher to adopt who might claim to work against the oppression of disabled people – the task was that of going beyond those terms: it was *one of changing the terms of debate*.

This is a highly political act: to reframe a perception of a situation – though this is not to reduce politics (which are about contests[6] or struggles) to language and ideas. How language is used matters (Fulcher, 1989) but it is not all that matters. Changing the terms of debate is a tactic which may give temporary advantage: '. . . each state of the social world is thus no more than a temporary equilibrium' (Bourdieu, 1990, p. 141).

I should emphasize that all of this pondering of method and tactic was half conscious. The clarity is something I have put on the process retrospectively (so that was what I did!). At the time it was a struggle – first, conceptualizing tasks and tactics, or method as we've been taught to call it – as I cooked a meal, swam, drove a car, went to sleep, my mind was grappling with questions. How can I get across the notions of struggle, contradiction and dilemmas, and the limits of a managerial approach to government policy practices? How can I persuade to a more complex view than the situation and its attendant emotions of frustration have been simplistically constructed? I knew the discursive practices had to be challenged but I would have to do it in a way which would not lose the audiences. I lived the research process in a way none of the decision-making models nor 'plans' for research can convey or capture. This is not to claim an 'heroic' research act but to intimate the layers of consciousness which are at work in undertakings when we involve ourselves in them. What I now see I worked towards was a report whose form was more like that of a condensed teaching course: a number of topics would have to be covered, key questions posed and central issues queried and exposed. I would work by raising questions: the quintessential starting point for teaching, and by making contrasts (the Socratic method). There was no time for, nor could I be conclusive about, highly technical controversies or 'knowledges'. The traditional academic method or treatise of summary argument and thesis, disposing of an alternate argument, would not do: that could not persuade and, as method which seeks to be 'authoritative', it would require several treatises since the technical areas were vast.

I would therefore pose questions rather than make authoritative statements; I would challenge the taken-for-granted 'expert' assumptions (this is the quintessential sociological task – Berger and Luckman, 1967) by somehow revealing the limits of their authority. Later I was to find I would do this by carefully juxtaposing key quotations from each of the authorities. Later, too, I was to find that I could present the differing accounts of policy – the one rational and managerial (the 1990s' rendering of liberal philosophy) and the other, a political-theoretical discussion, as tales. The differences between these had been a query which kept surfacing in my thoughts: how to present it?

GATHERING

I had 25 days for the project. I began with the idea of 'communication', setting aside the further topic of 'communicating with' severely disabled people, and aiming to provide a context for it.

The 'specialists' or experts in Melbourne on 'communication' are speech therapists and psychologists, predominantly in tertiary institutions, and a very much smaller number of alternative practitioners in facilitated communication, as well as one government programme called SCIOP (annually funded). I used the phone, asked for key references, picked up the central issues of 'augmentative and alternative' communication, read Biklen (1990), started to read (much later when I got a copy) *Annie's Coming Out* and went to libraries, not on a computer search but with clues on cards: references suggested and found, serendipitously, some highly apposite texts, including Raymond Williams' book on communicating, bought the latest text for parents by two leading Melbourne speech pathologists, rang the Communication Disorders Department of the former Health Sciences Institute, now part of a university, and visited DEAL (the Dignity, Education and Learning centre, known for the work of Rosemary Crossley and others) three times, and SCIOP once, scanned a journal called *AAC* and related texts. Most people I called were extremely helpful. These were my main materials. And though I did not realize it at the time when I read them, only weeks before, three other books were major influences in shaping my thinking on how to write: these were Richard Rorty's essays (1991a; 1991b) and Isabel Allende's (1991) *The Stories of Eva Luna*.

I met with the recreation workers, with the senior lecturer, sensed their frustration, saw they, the workers, expected little to come of this project and continued my pondering: how to convey a sociological view of their position, the public spaces in which they now worked. How to translate what they saw as personal troubles (governments say do this and we're meant to implement but it's difficult) to public issues,[7] how to expose the limits of ideas in policy of need and choice, and to bring to the forefront of their thinking complex issues about the nature of political responsibility, government and policy practices in the 1990s. The senior lecturer and I had only brief conversations; his brief to the project was succinct but not directive and, with the article or two he sent on autonomy and philosophical matters, I could both read and sense his concerns.

The task of writing for and persuading public servants, for some reason, I saw as more daunting, my view perhaps informed by a level of despair in the face of the now rapidly dominant discourse in government and bureaucratic arenas of managerialism, an approach which Stephen Ball (1990) stringently critiques. I had had firsthand experience of that discourse, and its associated nonsenses, as they can be, just when that discourse was beginning to be deployed in a large, traditional agency: yet two of us had created a small space for people with sight loss to construct new policy practices as they wanted them. This undertaking had reaffirmed that policy is made at all levels, and brought with it optimism.

I met with a senior public servant and sensed her genuine concerns that recreation policy would 'integrate' severely disabled people through these leisure programmes the department funded, and started struggling with the task. I took away the department's policy document: brief, and it was, as they say, under review anyway (the monies for the project were from the Department of Sport and Recreation), read the two Canadian books on integration and leisure which the department then saw as their 'bible'. As I imagined, both books adopted a merely rational approach to developing recreation policy to integrate the severely disabled: it was a matter of principles and working with the idea of normalization.

As I gathered, I also pondered on how to write, how to engage these diverse audiences, briefly and persuasively in a way that argument and counterargument not only would not – engage or persuade – but would also take too much time, and require impossible research or authority on my part. At the least, such a method would require, it seemed to me, 'facts' about the topic of communicating, for instance. I would, instead, expose as much as I could about the topics and their issues: search their assumptions, for the central motif which would reveal them, their limits, their nuances, what each had excluded. I would present these approaches as 'tales'. This would be a central writing strategy. Tales would raise issues, stand in contrast to another and expose the limits of their authority. 'Tales?' you may say, 'But this is postmodern twaddle!'

WRITING

I began by setting the scene: telling the tale of a recreation worker on the way to a weekly meeting with her 'clients' in an agency, imagining her reflections and their attendant emotions, and immediately raising questions about who had constituted this public space. Thus I shifted the focus from that scene to politicians, public servants, agency managers and academics who teach the workers. I asked how each of these 'actors' present their ideas and action (or how they represent their discursive practices) as 'rational'. By the second page, I had raised the ideas of responsibility in policy (a crucial dimension; Hindess, 1986), and of policy at all levels, and had put some question marks around the idea of 'rational' action. These ideas would become central problematics in the text which I could then engage with in later chapters.

I took the young woman's reflections further, including her view that her clients 'can't speak' (the recreation worker was fictional but typical but not representative of all recreation workers): yet (rational) government policy tells her not to deploy a deficit model. 'The young woman's head spins with these contradictions.' That allowed me to introduce a further central theme: that of contradictions and dilemmas in social life. That, too, was to be a central concept, or tool, or tactic, in persuading the reader to reflect more broadly on the public space in which the recreation worker was so intimately engaged. I wrote next on the idea of communicating.

On communicating

I began uncontentiously: What do authorities say? But I was clearly asking subtextual questions about 'authority'. I chose quotations to reveal the assumptions of the authors which thereby became limitations from another perspective. I drew on eight sources: on local speech pathologists, two of whom provided a model of communication as mechanical, pass-the-parcel messages; Raymond Williams (1981) – wonderfully useful for the idea of literacy as struggle within and across cultures but limited too, in some of its cultural assumptions; a neurophysiological text from a Victorian university which was open about the limits of our knowledge of the brain's functioning; academics who drew on Piaget's developmental model; Basil Bernstein; and argument too, influenced here by Isabel Allende and Jenny Corbett's writings, and by another sociologist of education (Winter, 1991), that communicating belongs to the 'heart and the eye'. Each of these sources was, I wrote, a tale and the differences between them showed that 'ideas about communication are highly contested' (thus introducing another idea central to my thesis). Thus I was able to argue that 'Communication is inseparable from the *culture* in which it occurs: it is based in people's *limited knowledges* and in the broader *culture(s)* (such as the deaf culture, or social class) to which someone belongs. Moreover, communicating relies on complex neurophysiological process and structures which are little understood' (Fulcher, 1992, p. 11). By this method of writing I sought to raise questions well beyond those texts or views considered in isolation, to open a space in the reader's mind where the matters were wider and more problematic than he or she had thought and thereby to start a process of self-reflexivity. Thus I set out concepts which I assumed the reader, whatever his or her position, or from whichever audience he or she came, would not readily bring to the topic of communication. In my gathering I had tested this assumption: it had not been refuted.

This provided the context for discussing the topic of communicating and severely disabled people. It showed the prior controversies over communication in general: I could then pose questions about communicating with severely disabled people, beyond those which emerge from a narrow focus which might see the issues as purely technical and as specific to these struggles. I outlined three approaches in Victoria to communicating and severely disabled people, and I began by describing their institutional bases (their sources of funding, their status, their stability of funding), including some brief historical details,

outlining some of their central ideas and describing their approaches to
severely disabled people and the issue of choice. I contrasted the well funded
academic approaches with the tenuously funded activities at DEAL. I juxta-
posed the academic concern with assessment and professional decisions, at the
same time, quoting at length a text which revealed the unspoken dilemmas in
reaching clear decisions (the continuing problem in a rational decision-making
model), with the ideas of augmentative, alternative and facilitated communication, which are the approaches of both DEAL and SCIOP, though in different
ways. Through apt quotations I was able to develop the ideas already
presented, to put the idea of a 'common language community', to question the
idea of linguistic competence, its profound cultural biases, and to query the
idea of 'language', as we generally understand that, in the developmental
model, as culturally relative.

The neurophysiological text allowed me to suggest that severely disabled
people who have not had the opportunity to develop their language skills
while they were young have had reduced opportunities to develop their
innate abilities. Thus I could ask: What does this say about 'choice'? Can we
think of choice without thinking of a person's past life chances, of
opportunities they may not have had? Neurophysiological research also
reportedly tells us that the brain, when faced with new situations, continues
to develop. What does this say about the idea of unable to learn? I sought to
show the cultural relativity of the practices in Victoria surrounding facilitated
communication: its lack of acceptance compared with some places in the
USA[8].

By now I had intimated the ideas which would inform the report's recommendations. I had also posed another central idea, that of culture, and in
asking not what do we know, but what is clear, I could say that

> The history of various forms of literacy shows us that communicating is
> based in *struggles* and that communicating is a *complex, interactive
> process*[9]. Where people communicate they are not, metaphorically,
> passing a parcel from one person to one another: communicating involves
> complex cultural interactions where there are levels of understanding and
> misunderstanding, always. Seeing communicating as cultural interactions
> suggests the idea of *cultures of communicating*. Deaf people claim their
> speechless ways of communicating are a language in its own right and a
> culture they (but not others) value. A psychologist suggests that we should
> see autistic children, who can use computers and communicate with one
> another, as a *sub-culture*. This cultural view suggests that, when we fail to
> understand what someone else is trying to convey and when they fail to
> understand what we're trying to get across, rather than impose a judg-
> ment of 'deficient!', we should see this gap as a *cultural divide*. Adopting
> this concept does not mean that we ignore differences in neurally-based
> motor processes and in styles of 'communicating'. The idea of *cultural*

divide means that we should take into account much more than a 'single' approach to communicating might suggest.

(Fulcher, 1992, p. 31)

I summarized:

[The] idea that communication difficulties are one-sided and belong to the individual with a severe disability . . . is . . . *not culturally literate*. A different idea has been suggested: that there is a *cultural gap in communication: a cultural divide* between the person with a severe disability and others, such as recreation workers. The idea of a one-sided deficit is also *ahistorical* in that it ignores the historical struggle of different groups to gain literacy. Some reference has been made to the *historical struggle for literacy*, both within societies, and between them. Recent contests over the Australian media belong in this history as do the Victorian struggles surrounding communication and people with severe disabilities.

(ibid., p. 36).

I wrote next on policy.

On policy

I set out, first, a liberal, rational reading of government disability policy, both the Commonwealth Disability Services Act 1986, and its counterpart, the Victorian Disability Services Act 1991, suggesting that this reading is how government presents it: how it would like us to think about it. Its terms of discourse ineluctably do this: principles, objectives, outcomes (the linear, normative, rational view of policy). I had already, in the preface, questioned this view of policy by quoting a British journal I could describe as relatively conservative, thereby implying that an unproblematic reading of a discourse of principles, objectives, outcomes was even more conservative:

Government social policy is not now – and never has been – based on rational analysis or on any one coherent and consistent set of principles. For better or worse, discussions of what principles should determine social provision are not likely to be very productive. What motivates social action is less rational analysis than motives both base and noble.

(Piachaud, 1991)

I spelt out the principles in both the 1986 and 1991 Acts, making the point that these were presented as social justice and as economic rationalism and that they contained discourses of rights and of participation, and of individualism: ideas of independence, achievement, individual capacities, lifestyles, needs, supports and goals. As well, the Commonwealth Act's vocabulary 'contains themes of professional assessment'. I suggested both Acts can be read as models of liberal, humane legislation and as providing a guide to principles for recreation programmes (for disabled people). I suggested that

> . . . the legislation (and the associated policy documents) proclaim a *rational* world: that decisions made at other levels – by public servants, agency managers, recreation workers – will be made with reason. Decisions are a central concept in the rational world view. The 1986 legislation purports – as the political culture of western democracies generally purport – that the legislation and associated policy is received into a community of autonomous individuals who can be governed by their rational consent [Hindess, 1991b]. Thus the legislation and policy documents are silent on the *contests* which surround disability. Chapter 7 discusses principles based in these silences. But Chapter 8 discusses these contests.
>
> (Fulcher, 1992, p. 44)

I discussed the Department of Sport and Recreation's policy and its key documents (including Hutchinson and Lord, 1979), suggesting that these shared the position of the Commonwealth 1986 and Victorian 1991 legislation, and that its idea of integration was largely interpreted as 'place' (*at* a football match, etc.), and as based on 'norms and patterns in the community (normalization as the underlying idea)'. I wrote that the ideas of principles and objectives have a more complex relation to practice than the rational model of policy would suggest: that they belong to much wider debates on morality and politics, and that these debates are central to social policy and to political theory (Fulcher, 1992, p. 56).

Drawing on quotations which prefaced the report (Disability is not about wheelchairs; Disability is *disputed* (Fulcher, 1989), and '. . . definitions of disability are only preliminary skirmishes in these contests' (Chap. 5 of the report)), and on earlier accounts (Hindess, 1986; Fulcher, various), I wrote a political tale of disability policy. From this stance, the rational tale of policy is silent on the contests which constitute politics and which surround disability (at whatever level, whether in schools or in agencies, for instance). I pointed out the contradictions in disability policy which are elided by simple renderings of ideas like 'choice': I may choose that my son, in an institutional 'cottage' for the intellectually disabled, go to DEAL once a week to learn facilitated communication, but I am a pensioner and no transport is provided for the journey of several miles. Or, I may choose, as a severely disabled person, to be with others like me. (What does this do to the idea of integration as 'place', I could ask?) I may find integration (solidarity with others) in an institution (as in Alan Bennett's chief character in the radio play, *A Lady of Letters*). Thus I could argue that '. . . the connections between the ideas of "choice" and "consumer", two central ideas in current disability policy, can encourage images of "equally free" supermarket consumers: a construct of a free-floating actor, devoid of biographical history and opportunities' (Fulcher, 1992, p. 65). I pointed out that

Government-level policy is silent on the contradictions between recreation or leisure policy and progams which are meant to achieve 'consumer outcomes': where the conditions for communication are absent: where neither the recreation worker can understand the other person, and the person with a severe disability may not be able to respond or convey their wish.

(ibid.)

and that the rational view of policy, as in professional language, masks its politics. I noted that a political tale of policy may be rejected

. . . as critical, counterproductive, pessimistic, a conspiracy theory, as offering no obvious solutions. These objections may be deployed by various policy actors and for a variety of objectives. But the outcomes of this political tale – the results of deploying this model – are not foregone conclusions.

Politics as contests have no given actors, no given forms and no predetermined outcomes (Wickham, unpublished: 20).

(Fulcher, 1992, p. 6)

In place of ethics and principles, I talked of morals and politics and of the *cultural politics of disability*, drawing on Jenny Corbett's (1991) wonderfully brief piece to show that normality is contested. Then I could ask: Is Australian culture different in its cultural politics?

At this point, I inserted a chapter consisting only of quotations: as 'personal tales', the tale that shaped this tactic being Isabel Allende's 'The Road North'. In this story, the South American grandfather, when asked by his daughter how they could bring up her deaf son, replied 'With patience . . . It's a thing of eye, time and heart'. So he trained (but without its Anglo-Saxon connotations) his deaf grandson 'to look out for himself'. A Romantic discourse, you may say, only in a Eurocentric view of culture.

In summing up this strategic view of policy (as opposed to a wider political theoretical discussion about the nature of politics), I was able to suggest that the 'specific site model of policy' had its uses. Finally, the report recommended that both severely disabled Victorians and recreation workers needed opportunities to learn about modes and aspects of communication they may not know about, and that '. . . only when these opportunities have been provided and fully explored, can the responsibility or onus of "choice" in recreation programs, as it is presently conveyed in current government leisure and disability policy, be relocated by government to individual recreation workers and to Victorians with severe disabilities' (Fulcher, 1992, p. 92). It also sought to replace the idea of economic productivity as the only source of social cohesion with that of *cultural productivity*:

These ideas on the *cultural politics of disability* suggest that culturally productive recreation activities can achieve solidarity between people with severe disabilities and others, and that these activities may thus reduce the exclusion that people with severe disabilities, individually, so frequently experience. They also suggest that, in some limited contexts we might call a community, culturally productive recreation activities might transform some of the political structures which systematically maintain this exclusion.

(ibid., p. 78)

Thus the report recommended both that the idea of integration in recreation and leisure policy practices with severely disabled Victorians be replaced by the idea of 'cultural productivity' and that such recreation programmes have a high priority. These were the changed terms of debate for policy I had struggled with in the 13 weeks' half-time work in 1991 and 1992.

WHAT HAD I DONE?

Had the research changed or qualified my assumptions? Had I taken the research terms for granted? Had my writing changed the community's understanding of this area? These are the questions the editors ask of me in prodding me to my conclusions!

To the first, I can answer 'No'. I remain as I have been since earlier analyses (Fulcher, 1986; 1989) both profoundly ambivalent about the contribution of research to this field and somehow convinced that, with care, at the right moment, given due space, tenuous as this may be, that research can momentarily clarify the various encounters which characterize what we call special educational needs. Such research, if sufficiently self-conscious and critical, may help suspend the analyses with which many will enter these encounters, perhaps reframe their frameworks in political not exhortatory terms. But such research, if it is to counter the dominant readings, must be political in a broad sense. That is, it must locate its concepts, its theorizing, within a serious attempt to grapple with the political character of the modern West, to use Hindess's phrase. It must therefore run the risks which such analysis provokes. It must retain a critical distance from, rather than adopt the stance of accommodation with, governance. Such an analysis had been my aim. Beyond this ambivalence, this brief project of some 13 half-time weeks in the southern summer of 1991 to 1992 gave me a personal tool: that complex topics, even in truncated time, if given a free run, can yield to disciplined analysis.

Had I taken the research terms for granted? My answer is also 'No'. It is hard to imagine how a sociologist cannot retain a critical distance from the categories of policy and of medicine. Grappling with the politics of categories has persuaded me of the necessity for political analyses. Without such analyses, the researcher engaged in policy work remains a policy analyst (as, to some extent, I had been despite struggles against this, in 1983–4): hostage to the social seductions of political intrigues in what we call the policy-making process (in this case, the intrigues around a review table), to the impossibility of serious intellectual work in such a setting, to attenuated analyses. One is paid to assist in the task of government? And yet, even in affecting government-level decisions or the decisions of those who work with them, the analyses may offer a political advantage until the politics shift.

Had my writing changed the community's understanding of this area? This had been my objective. By the end of the report I had contended with five aspects of policy: against the dominant discourse on integration, as it had emerged by the 1990s; against the dominant discourse or understanding of the nature of policy; against a view of deficient individuals and their 'needs'; against a simplistic rendering of choice in policy; and against a false view of responsibility. I had not been prescriptive. I wanted people to suspend the analyses they brought to the encounters between the so-called able-bodied and the severely disabled. To do this, they needed to be reflective. So had I created self-reflexivity? Had I thereby changed the political terms of debate? Had I modified '. . . the categories of thought which help to orient individual and collective practices and in particular the categories through which distortions are perceived and appreciated' (Bourdieu, 1990, p. 141)? And, further, had I changed the focus of concern, from individual recreation workers and their frustrations, to a concern with the nature of government-level policy practices and the idea of government level responsibility? Had I thereby shifted the concern of the workers to a focus on the politics of government policy practices? It seems I might.

It is mid-1993 and the phone rings again. Stage 2 of the project may now get underway. The fax refers to stage 1, describing the task of the report I wrote as that of

> . . . conceptualising the question of communication with respect to people with severe disabilities. The particular focus of this work was that of recreation and the role of the recreation worker. The outcome of that project was the report: *PICK UP THE PIECES! What do recreation workers need to know about policy and working with people with severe disabilities?*

> That report has been the subject of considerable discussion, especially among workers in the severe disability field, and among interested academics. The ideas on which it is based have created a great deal of interest, and in some cases anxiety, in terms of their far reaching implications for radical change. Such change is directed not only at what is to be done, but also at what constitutes appropriate goals, and indeed at how the fundamental questions of choice, recreation, and communication are to be thought about.

> (Trowbridge, personal communication)

Tales, then, have some consequences?

NOTES

1. DPI Australia use the terminology 'person with a disability'. For this chapter, in a UK text, I have adopted the English usage except in quoting from the report.
2. On the nature of the monitoring culture, see Power (1992).
3. Cohen (1985).
4. An educator, discussing the new 'multimedia', where the idea of information was the dominant concept: '. . . you can integrate texts, bird calls . . . all this information' (ABC *Science Show*, 29 May 1993).
5. 'The waning of the social and political conflict in the "real" sphere finds its appropriate counterpart in the intellectual and artistic fields with the evanescence of the genuine critical spirit. This spirit . . . can only exist in and through the establishment of a distance with what there is, entailing the conquest of a point of view beyond the given, therefore a work of creation. The present period is thus best defined as the general retreat into conformism' (Castoriadis, 1992, p. 22).
6. Wickham (unpublished).
7. C. Wright Mills's (1970) classic distinction.
8. Although it is, for instance, a highly controversial practice in, for example, New York State.
9. It is also structured: typically, this means imposed.

REFERENCES AND FURTHER READING

Allende, I. (1991) *The Stories of Eva Luna*. Penguin Books, Harmondsworth.
Ball, S. J. (1990) 'Management as moral technology: a Luddite analysis', in S. J. Ball (ed.) *Foucault and Education: Disciplines and Knowledge*, Routledge, London, pp. 153–66.
Barton, L. (1986) 'The politics of special education needs', *Disability, Handicap and Society*, Vol. 1, no. 3, pp. 273–90.
Barton, L. and Tomlinson, S. (eds) (1981) *Special Education: Policy, Practices and Social Issues*. Harper & Row, London.
Berger, P. L. and Luckmann, T. (1967) *The Social Construction of Reality*. Allen Lane, London.
Biklen, D. *et al.* (1991) 'I amn not A Utistivc on thje Typ ('I'm not Autistic on the Typewriter', *Disability, Handicap and Society*, Vol. 6, no. 3, pp. 161–80.
Bourdieu, P. (1990) *The Logic of Practice*. Polity Press, Cambridge.
Castoriadis, C. (1992) 'The reteat from autonomy: post-modernism as generalized conformism', *Thesis Eleven*, Vol. 31, pp. 14–23.
Cohen, S. (1985) *Visions of Social Control*. Polity Press, Cambridge.
Coldwell, R. A. (1991) 'Intellectually handicapped children: development of hieroglyphic symbols', *Australian Education Computing*, September.
Corbett, J. (1991) 'So, who wants to be normal?', *Disability, Handicap and Society*, Vol. 6, no. 3, pp. 259–60.
Corbett, J. (1992) 'Careful teaching: researching a special career', *British Journal of Educational Research*, Autumn.
Crossley, R. and McDonald, A. (1989 edn) *Annie's Coming Out*. Penguin Books Australia, Ringwood.
Foucault, M. (1977) *Discipline and Punish: The Birth of the Prison*. Penguin Books, Harmondsworth.

Fulcher, G. (1986) 'Australian policies on special education: towards a sociological account', *Disability, Handicap and Society*, Vol. 1, no. 1, pp. 19–52.

Fulcher, G. (1989) *Disabling Policies? A Comparative Approach to Education Policy and Disability*. Falmer Press, Lewes.

Fulcher, G. (1990a) 'Policy practice and social theory: towards an agenda', in A. Jamrozik (ed.) *Social Policy in Australia: What Future for the Welfare State? Proceedings of the National Social Policy Conference*. Sydney, 5–7 July.

Fulcher, G. (1990b) 'Students with special needs: lessons from comparisons', *Journal of Education Policy*, Vol. 5, no. 4, pp. 347–58.

Fulcher, G. (1992) *Pick Up the Pieces! What Do Recreation Workers Need to Know about Policy and Working with People with Severe Disabilities?* Report prepared for the Department of Leisure and Recreation, Phillip Institute of Technology, Bundoora, Victoria, February.

Fulcher, G. (1993) 'Schools and contests: a reframing of the effective schools debate?', in R. Slee (ed.) *The Politics of Integration in Australia*. Falmer Press, Lewes.

Hewitt, M. (1983) 'Biopolitics and social policy: Foucault's account of welfare', *Theory, Culture and Society*, Vol. 2, no. 1, pp. 67–84.

Hindess, B. (1986) 'Actors and social relations', in M. L. Wardell and S. P. Turner (eds) *Sociological Theory in Transition*, Allen & Unwin, Boston, Mass., pp. 113–26.

Hindess, B. (1991a) 'Imaginary presuppositions of democracy', *Economy and Society*, Vol. 20, no. 2, pp. 73–95.

Hindess, B. (1991b) 'Power and rationality: the western concept of political community'. Paper presented at the Thesis Eleven Conference: Reason and Imagination, Monash University.

Hutchinson, P. and Lord, J. (1979) *Recreation Integration: Issues and Alternatives in Leisure Services and Community Involvement*. Ottawa, Leisurability Publications.

Miller, P. and Rose, N. (1990) 'Governing economic life', *Economy and Society*, Vol. 19, no. 1, pp. 1–31.

Piachaud, D. (1991) 'Social policy beyond the social services', *Policy Studies*, Vol. 12, no. 4, pp. 47–52.

Power, M. (1992) 'The audit society: monitoring as a technology of government'. Paper presented at the History of the Present workshop, 4 November.

Richardson, L. (1990) *Writing Strategies: Reaching Diverse Audiences*. Sage, Newbury Park.

Rorty, R. (1991a) *Objectivity, Relativism, and Truth. Philosophical Papers*, Vol. 1. Cambridge University Press.

Rorty, R. (1991b) *Essays on Heidegger and Others*, Vol. 2. Cambridge University Press.

Tomlinson, S. (1982) *A Sociology of Special Education*. Routledge, London.

Wickham, G. (unpublished) 'Justice, democracy and the demise of politics.'

Williams, R. (ed.) (1981) *Contact: Human Communication and its History*. Thames & Hudson, London.

Winter, R. (1991) 'Post-modern sociology as a democratic educational practice? Some suggestions', *British Journal of Sociology of Education*, Vol. 12, no. 4, pp. 467–81.

Wright Mills, C. (1970) *The Sociological Imagination*. Penguin Books, Harmondsworth.

POLICY DOCUMENTS

Integration in Victorian Education (1984) Report of the Ministerial Review of Educational Services for the Disabled. Melbourne, Government Printer (Chair: M. K. Collins).

General Manager, Southern Metropolitan Region, Office of Schools Administration, Ministry of Education, Victoria, *Integration Resource Allocations – 1991*, 176/1990, 12 December 1990.

Special Educational Needs (1978) Report of the Committee of Enquiry into the Education of Handicapped Children and Young People. London, HMSO (Warnock Report).

3

THE ETHICS OF POLICY-FOCUSED RESEARCH IN SPECIAL EDUCATIONAL NEEDS

Sheila Riddell, Sally Brown and Jill Duffield

INTRODUCTION

In this chapter we provide an account of our experience of researching policy and provision for children with specific learning difficulties. During the course of the project, which was commissioned by the Scottish Office Education Department, we were aware of two major and interconnecting influences on the research. The first concerned the way in which we conceptualized special educational needs, which was at variance with the views of some of the key groups in our study. The second concerned the pressures and conflicts which inevitability arise in the context of engaging in government-sponsored research.

It is worth commenting at this point on our understanding of special educational needs. As others (e.g. Oliver, 1990) have noted, much research in this area rests, either implicitly or explicitly, on a personal tragedy view. Educational problems and the responsibility for dealing with them are presumed to rest with the child and his or her family. We do not wish to deny that the nature of an individual's impairment affects their experience of disability, but feel it is important to emphasize that, as Abberley (1987) has argued, these are always mediated by political, historical and social conditions. In this way, a balance is struck between the traditional psychological view that the difficulty resides within the child and the interactionist view that disability must be understood as a social construction. Applying these ideas to specific learning difficulties was not straightforward and during our early team meetings we often found ourselves saying, 'Well what exactly do you mean by specific learning difficulties?' From our experience of teaching in school and university we all knew young people who appeared to have an unexplained gap between their rather poor literacy skills and their ability in other areas. At the same time, we had reservations about the Dyslexia Association's insistence that the condition is constitutional in origin and could and should be differentiated from other forms of learning difficulty. This account, we felt, depended on a fixed view of ability and at times was used to promote the belief that dyslexic children were more deserving of additional resources than other children with learning difficulties because they were more intelligent and therefore more salvageable. A British dyslexia leaflet, for instance, argued: 'Surely no nation can afford to waste such a precious asset as people with intelligence who are unable to reach their proper potential' (British Dyslexia Association, undated). In the study we present here, our research questions were certainly not designed to settle the ongoing debates among medics, psychologists and educationists concerning the origin and nature of dyslexia (see Pumfrey and Reason, 1991) nor to address the question of incidence. Rather, we wished to investigate the way in which different interest groups, particularly education authority personnel and parents, employed competing discourses in the discussion of dyslexia/specific learning difficulties as part of their struggle over resources. The methods we employed (mainly interviews and questionnaire surveys) were traditional, but the central thrust of the strategy was exploratory. In the conclusion we return to a consideration of the conceptualization of specific learning difficulties and special educational needs and highlight our central dilemma, that by researching specific learning difficulties we were in danger of reifying a construct whose existence and boundaries were strongly disputed. We discuss the strategies we employed to avoid such pressures and finally consider how our findings illuminate the intensifying struggle between competing interest groups in the present political climate.

The structure of the chapter is as follows. We begin by providing an overview of the origins of the project and the issues which must be addressed by those involved in government-sponsored policy-oriented research, particularly in controversial areas such as specific learning difficulties. Having outlined our general approach, we discuss the methods we adopted and our efforts to problematize specific learning difficulties at all stages in the research. Finally, we consider the way in which our findings have been interpreted and our understanding of the issues involved in researching special educational needs has developed during the course of the study.

THE ORIGINS OF THE PROJECT

In 1990 the Scottish Office Education Department (SOED) announced that it wished to commission a piece of research on specific learning difficulties with the following aims:

1. To describe current policies and practices for the recognition, identification, assessment and provision to meet the needs of children with specific learning difficulties.
2. To identify the criteria used, by providers and 'customers', to judge the effectiveness of different approaches.
3. To report on how current policies and practices perform in relation to these criteria.
4. To present this information in a way which informs and advises those who make decisions (particularly policy-makers, teachers and teacher educators) on how to deal with the problems of these children.

The specification reflected the usual practice of the Scottish Office that research should be tied very closely to policy-related matters and, as the research aims indicate, the government's concern to promote the account-ability of producers to consumers was very much in evidence. The project was to last for 18 months and the budget was £45,000. After some deliberation, Sheila Riddell and Sally Brown decided to submit a tender for the contract and were successful. Carole Ogilvy worked on the project for the first year of its life and Jill Duffield for the second. The findings are reported in Riddell *et al.,* 1992. At this point it should be noted that while the terms 'specific learning difficulties' and 'dyslexia' are sometimes used synonymously, each conveys particular understandings of the nature and origin of the problem. The use of terminology by different interest groups became a central focus of the research and is discussed in greater detail below.

Clearly, no research project is conceived in a political and social vacuum and a question which intrigued us was why this particular area had been prioritized by the Scottish Office. In Scotland there is a well established tradition of government-sponsored research and elaborate procedures are used to identify research priorities (Brown, 1993). The Research and Intelligence Unit, a division of the Scottish Office Central Research Unit, gathers views from HMI, administrators in the various divisions and a range of interested parties such as voluntary organizations. Members of Parliament may canvass the Secretary of State for Education, who also has a strong influence over decisions concerning the projects which should be funded. Government patronage of educational research in Scotland clearly has a number of advantages for the research community, particularly in the present context where great store is placed on attracting external funding to universities. However, the negative consequences were pointed up by Humes (1986) who maintained that the arrangements tended to foster a rather uncritical approach. He commented (p. 161):

> The funding arrangements for educational research in Scotland give what can only be described as an excessive measure of power to the SED, through RIU (Research and Intelligence Unit). It is not unreasonable that central government should determine *part* of an overall research

programme, but if research is to remain worthy of the name, it is important that some of those involved should not be dependent on centrally
controlled patronage.

Properly independent research, Humes concluded, might only be conducted by
those who eschewed SOED funding. Researchers in Scotland, then, may find
themselves in something of a double bind. Participation in funded research
projects is an important means of contributing to current educational debates.
However, there are attendant dangers that the receipt of government funding
may neutralize potentially critical voices.

In the Department of Education at Stirling University, we generally adopt a
pragmatic attitude to SOED funding, bidding for research projects in areas
which we feel have substantive and theoretical interest. We recognize that the
research is likely to be tightly associated with policy concerns and is expected
to have an impact on practice. If we are successful in winning a research
contract, we are aware that this means we must address the agenda which the
Scottish Office has set, but in addition we seek to highlight the theoretical
implications of the area of study in ways which are unlikely to have been envis-
aged in the research specification. We also make every effort to maintain our
critical perspective. If we judged that a piece of research had no interesting
theoretical or substantive spin-offs, or if it was merely being used to rubber-
stamp decisions which had already been made, then it is very unlikely that we
would bid for the work. Our approach might be seen as unhealthily pragmatic,
but we believe it allows us to take advantage of much-needed financial support
while maintaining the independence on which our credibility depends.
However, we are aware of the ethical issues which surround government-sponsored research and, within this context, the need to review constantly our
research strategies and methods. Above all, we need to pay attention to the
way in which research findings are used by interest groups once they are in the
public domain.

Given these concerns, it was important for us to understand the origins of
the project on specific learning difficulties. It appeared that the Scottish
Dyslexia Association had carried out a survey of its members which had
revealed considerable dissatisfaction among parents with the quality of
services provided by education authorities. This information had been
presented to the Secretary of State for Education, who had endorsed the view
of the Scottish Dyslexia Association that research should be commissioned
which would clarify current levels of provision and indicate future policy
developments. Another source of pressure on the Scottish Office was parents'
growing awareness of their legal rights. An increasing number of official
complaints were being received from parents of children with specific learning
difficulties concerning the lack of specialized provision available in schools.
Parliamentary lobbying was also being used and we were intrigued to note
that, in response to a parliamentary question on Monday 25 June 1990 on the

incidence of dyslexia and the nature of provision, Ian Lang, Secretary of State for Education, indicated that the problem was being addressed by a research project at Stirling University which would '. . . identify any gaps in provision and offer guidance to teachers of such children'. It appeared that the remit of the research was being stretched from analysing policy and provision to providing a future action plan. Generally, then, the origins of the research project seemed to lie in the determination of a number of groups to raise the profile of specific learning difficulties in order to chivy the government into action. The lobbying and delaying tactics which were evident in the parliamentary exchange referred to above served as a useful reminder at an early point in the research that we were going to have to work very hard at establishing our own agenda.

THE BASIS OF OUR RESEARCH BID TO THE SCOTTISH OFFICE

In the light of these layers of conflicting interests, we might have decided that the whole area was too politically charged for us to be able to research it in any meaningful way. On the other hand, one could argue that it is precisely in those areas where competing interest groups are jockeying for position that researchers may make a useful input in elucidating the issues. In deciding to conduct the research, we were clearly rejecting Humes's (1986) view that engaging in government-funded policy-oriented research almost inevitably leads to the production of poor-quality work.

By way of contrast, we found the arguments of Finch (1986) very helpful. She suggested four reasons why researchers should engage in policy-focused work and these are summarized below. First, at the most cynical level, it is increasingly the case that, in order to obtain research funds from government departments, charitable foundations or the research councils, policy relevance must be demonstrated. This situation is unlikely to change in the near future, particularly in the context of the 1993 government white paper mentioned earlier, which reasserted the government's insistence that publicly funded research must be able to demonstrate its relevance to wealth creation. Secondly, Finch noted that policy-oriented research has potential benefits for the development of knowledge, particularly in terms of focusing attention on the relatively powerful, a group which has often been neglected within social science research (Bell and Newby, 1977; Scott, 1984). Thirdly, Finch made the case that it is the responsibility of the social scientist to use his or her skills to contribute to the debate on contentious public issues. Finally and most compellingly, Finch argued that engagement with policy cannot be avoided. She noted:

Social scientists are de facto part of the social world which we study, and the knowledge which we produce can always potentially be used to some effect; therefore the idea that one can pursue a detached social science which does not engage with public issues is at best very naive.

(Finch, 1986, p. 3)

These views accorded with our sense that undertaking policy research should not be regarded a a second-best type of research activity. None the less, we were aware of the need to be clear of our value position which, as we indicated earlier, centred on the recognition that disabled people represent a socially disadvantaged group who are likely to experience downward social mobility during the course of their lives (Townsend, 1979; Walker, 1982). Given that, as Fulcher (1989) has argued, the discourses involved in constructing special educational needs play a crucial part in challenging or undermining this disadvantage, investigating divergent views of specific learning difficulties seemed likely to provide us with insight into wider policy struggles.

COMPETING DEFINITIONS OF SPECIFIC LEARNING DIFFICULTIES

Our initial review of the literature indicated the conceptual complexity of the area. First, it was evident that the way in which specific learning difficulties were construed was potentially at variance with official thinking on special educational need since the late 1970s. The Warnock Report (DES, 1978) rejected the use of statutory categories of handicap and substituted instead the notion of a continuum of learning difficulties which might be experienced by 20 per cent of children at some point during their educational career. Warnock felt that the idea of a sharp disjunction between those who experienced learning difficulties and others was misguided. She also recommended that learning difficulties should be seen as arising out of the interaction between the child and his or her environment. In place of the system of rigid classification, Warnock was moving towards a social constructionist view of learning difficulties (Oliver, 1988), although later on in the report categories of difficulty, such as visual, hearing and specific learning difficulties, are discussed. This suggests that, while promoting a view of learning difficulties as perceptually based, Warnock wished to retain a view of certain difficulties as residing within the child. The progress report of Scottish HMI (SED, 1978) probably went further than Warnock in terms of adopting a social constructionist perspective. This report suggested that, for slow learners in mainstream schools, instead of locating the source of the problem as resting within the child, inappropriate curricula and teaching methods were more likely to be at fault. Rather than providing remedial teaching for these children in separate departments, the mainstream class teacher, assisted by the learning support teacher, should accept prime responsibility for their education. Both the Warnock and HMI reports were welcomed by education authorities and incorporated into their policy documents relatively rapidly.

British Dyslexia Association publications indicated that, far from endorsing these policy developments, their understanding of specific difficulties was firmly rooted within a medical model of disability, with the source of the difficulty located within the child. Although the British Dyslexia Association is prepared to use the term specific learning difficulties, the term 'dyslexia' is preferred, which is defined as

> A specific difficulty in learning, constitutional in origin, in one or more of reading, spelling and written language, which may be accompanied by difficulty in number work. It is particularly related to mastering and using a written language (alphabetic, numerical and musical notation) although often affecting oral language to some degree.

(Auger, 1990)

Assessments of the impact of the Warnock Report had frequently claimed that, despite its inconsistencies, one of its strengths was to undermine the established system of categorization whose function was to legitimize the exclusion of increasing numbers of children from mainstream education. Heward and Lloyd-Smith (1991, p. 21) noted, for example: 'The Warnock Committee set out a framework for the redirection of special educational policy away from its deeply institutionalized practice of categorization and segregation towards greater flexibility and integration, a policy long commended by advocates of better education for the handicapped.' There was evidently conflict between post-Warnock learning policy and the position of the British Dyslexia Association and clarifying the nature of this divide became the central focus of our work.

RESEARCH METHODS

Social science research methods are not neutral but themselves shape the way in which the world is construed. It is therefore important for researchers to be clear about the assumptions underlying their choice of methods. Such discussion has been evident in recent years in politically sensitive areas such as gender (Oakley, 1981; Finch, 1984; Riddell, 1989) and 'race' (Troyna and Carrington, 1989). Some writers like Oakley argued that when one woman is interviewing another, the prime concern must be to equalize the relationship as much as possible by engaging with the interviewee rather than treating her as an object to be manipulated. Finch (1984) commented on the quality of data which is likely to emerge when real rather than contrived empathy is present. On the other hand she warned of the dangers of exploitation which may arise in a situation which, despite the best intentions of the researcher, is fundamentally unequal. Whereas many women have seen the act of talking to another

woman as in tune with feminist thinking because of its potential at least ostensibly to equalize the balance of power between the researcher and the
researched, others such as Jayaratne (1983) have defended the use of survey
methods since these are likely to inform political action and are more likely to
be taken seriously by policy-makers. Troyna and Carrington's central concern
has been to explore ways in which anti-racist research may contribute to the
challenging of racism. In addition, they highlighted some incipient dangers in
work which sought to be anti-racist but which actually reinforced racist attitudes by reinforcing stereotypes or providing the state with essential data
which might be used to maintain racial inequalities.

By way of contrast, in the area of special needs, it is evident that little attention has been paid to the ethics of research, although, as in the area of 'race'
and gender, key questions demand attention such as the way in which parti-
sanship may be reconciled with the production of research which is rigorous
and convincing. In addition, there is the question, raised above, concerning
whether qualitative methods are intrinsically more appropriate for investigating social-justice issues because of the claim that they are more democratic.
Interestingly, Barnes (1991) rejected this argument, explaining: 'Unlike
previous studies of disability this book does not provide detailed case studies
documenting the isolated experiences of individual disabled people . . . This is
because such an approach tends to focus the reader's attention upon individual
disabled people, and not upon the discriminatory policies and institutionalized
practices which create disability.' In selecting our research methods, our
central concern, as sketched earlier, was to gain a handle on the way in which
different groups construed specific learning difficulties and the blueprints for
action which sprang from these views. We therefore decided to use the major
part of our resources to carry out interview and questionnaire surveys of key
players in the area (education authority personnel, parents, secretaries of local
branches of the Dyslexia Association, teacher educators, learning support
teachers and preservice teachers). Policy was also explored through the
analysis of key national and local documents and discussions with officers of
important administrative bodies such as the Scottish Examinations Board.
Some observation of aspects of specialized provision such as reading centres
was carried out, but we felt that focusing our energy on case studies of individual children and families would have diverted attention away from the
elucidation of policy. However, had we had more resources, we would have
wished to investigate learning support in action to illuminate the findings of
our policy study.

Our methods, then, were traditional in the sense that they adopted the
conventions of social science and were geared towards understanding the
perspectives of key players in the process of policy formation. Some
researchers, e.g. Lather (1991), would argue that research should always
involve the researcher engaging in the process of consciousness-raising and the
quest for emancipation. Any other research involves the imposition of meaning

by the researcher, an unacceptable use of power. Although recognizing the validity of the type of research advocated by Lather, we would argue that it is only one of a number of possible alternatives. Our work was intended to illuminate wider policy developments and, we hoped, would be of use to people with disabilities and their advocates. We were aware that our chosen methods involved the researcher mediating and interpreting the views of others, implying a responsibility to analyse and present the data in as honest and rigorous a way as possible. However, we recognized that our account represented only one version of the truth and that other researchers might reach different conclusions.

PROBLEMATIZING THE CONCEPT OF SPECIFIC LEARNING DIFFICULTIES

As we have argued throughout this chapter, given the political context of the project and the interest groups which stood to gain or lose from the outcomes, our major challenge was to retain a critical perspective throughout. This was underlined for us in the early stages of the project when permission to undertake research in a large urban region was initially withheld. The assistant director with responsibility for special needs explained that (1) there was resentment that the Scottish Office seemed to assume that regions would automatically agree to participate in its sponsored research; and (2) there were doubts about the political motivation of the project. In this particular region there was considerable opposition towards the recognition of specific learning difficulties as a separate category and the previous year there had been an angry exchange on a Radio Scotland programme between an educational psychologist, who felt that specific learning difficulties represented a middle-class neurosis, and a member of the Scottish Dyslexia Association, who was horrified at his attitude. In order to gain access to this region, the research team had to argue convincingly that they were not simply adopting the perspective of the Dyslexia Association, but were subjecting this to critical scrutiny.

The first phase of the project involved an interview survey with principal educational psychologists, education officers with responsibility for special needs and special needs advisers. In devising our interview schedule, we realized that specific learning difficulties might be construed as covering almost any aspect of special educational needs and we needed some indication of whether our interviewers would be covering common ground. To this end, we sent out a preliminary sheet of basic questions to principal psychologists to ascertain the range of difficulties which should be included under the heading of specific learning difficulties and the type they considered to be most salient. The majority described problems in the area of reading, writing and spelling as being the most significant and we therefore decided that the focus of the interviews would be on the area of literacy. In our interviews and questionnaires, we began by asking our respondents to explain their understanding of specific learning difficulties and we found that their replies were closely connected to their views on appropriate forms of assessment and provision.

Problematizing specific learning difficulties posed particular difficulties when it came to drawing up a sample of parents. It was evident that the Scottish Dyslexia Association was very happy to co-operate with the research and would be willing to supply the names of members. Although we wanted to include such parents in our sample, they were unlikely to be typical of all parents whose children might be identified as having specific learning difficulties. We therefore decided that half our sample should be contacted through local branches of the Scottish Dyslexia Association and the other half should be contacted through regional psychological services. The interviews conducted earlier with education authority personnel indicated that this part of the sampling procedure was unlikely to be straightforward for the following reasons:

- There was no agreed definition of specific learning difficulties across different authorities nor, in certain instances, within the same authority.
- Some authorities had adopted what we had termed an 'anti-categorization' approach to learning difficulties. In these authorities the emphasis was on meeting the needs of individual children rather than classifying them according to the nature or origin of their learning difficulties.
- In some authorities a degree of hostility was evident to the use of the term 'specific learning difficulties'. We suspected that these authorities were unlikely to be helpful in assisting us in compiling a sample.

Principal educational psychologists were asked to provide us with a list of parents 'whose children were identified as having specific learning difficulties' and, as we had anticipated, the ease with which they were able to do this reflected to some extent their conceptualization of special educational needs. One principal educational psychologist wrote, after consulting the special needs adviser: 'We are agreed that the way learning support is delivered here simply does not fit the bipolar structure you offer.' He noted that the submissions made to the Scottish Examinations Board for special examination arrangements normally indicated that the child experienced 'specific learning difficulties' or 'specific learning difficulties of a dyslexic or similar nature'. However, these diagnoses were simply used to obtain special examination dispensations and had not been discussed with parents, who might be greatly alarmed to hear that their children had been classified in this way. Another psychologist who felt unable to identify any parents of children with specific learning difficulties explained:

> The psychological service and learning support do not dichotomize youngsters as having specific or general difficulty in learning. In each instance the most appropriate strategy for responding to a youngster's educational need

is developed and a detailed description . . . is kept for that purpose. The categorizing you requested would require reconsideration of individual pupil records [and this could not be made without undue] investment of staff time.

Although most authorities were able to provide us with the names of parents whose children had been identified as experiencing specific learning difficulties, the fact that a minority were unable to do so meant that our sample had to be regarded as illustrative rather than representative. Different conceptualizations of specific learning difficulties were also evident in the response rate of learning support teachers. In regions where no distinction was drawn between specific and general difficulties, the response rate was much poorer than in regions where specific learning difficulties had a higher profile.

Clearly, children with special educational needs do not represent an absolute group since definitions depend on professional judgements and political factors. This underlines the importance of recognizing that research in this area cannot provide an objective view of reality, although it can provide insight into the way in which the world is construed. We have tried to reflect this view in our writing.

RESEARCH FINDINGS

We were aware that a number of groups had a particular interest in the outcome of our research, hoping that it would lend support to their position. The Scottish Dyslexia Association, for instance, was optimistic that by providing independent evidence of high levels of parental dissatisfaction, additional pressure could be placed on central government and education authorities to provide additional resources. Education authorities, on the other hand, were anxious that their practice should be vindicated and that the research would not support further calls from the dyslexia lobby on their already tightly stretched budgets. Bearing in mind this context, we thought carefully about the implications of our findings and how they should be presented.

To summarize, we noted that even though almost everyone recognized that some children might have particular difficulties with reading, writing and spelling, these were construed variously. Two broadly distinctive conceptualizations emerged from our respondents' accounts. Some felt children with specific learning difficulties should be identified as a separate group, whose problems were qualitatively different from those of other children. This we termed the discrete group view. Others felt that it was impossible to distinguish between specific and global learning difficulties and that all learning difficulties should be regarded as occurring along a continuum. This was termed the continuum view. Although it was theoretically possible to define boundaries on the continuum which would distinguish children with specific learning difficulties from others, most professionals felt it was almost impossible to do this in pratice. Among education authority personnel who supported a continuum view of learning difficulties, a minority expressed strong political opposition to drawing distinctions between different types of difficulty, since this focused attention on individual pupils rather than systemic problems. We termed this the anti-categorization view.

Those regarding children as a discrete group favoured psychometric forms of assessment and specialist tuition on a one-to-one or small group basis, whereas others felt that the needs of children with specific learning difficulties could be met by the mainstream teacher assisted by the learning support teacher using the type of teaching methods and materials which would be suitable for any child with literacy problems. Assessment should normally be on the basis of observation of normal classroom activity. Major contrasts emerged among the dominant education authority perspective, the continuum view and the perspectives of parents and voluntary organizations, who favoured the discrete group view and were highly critical of the refusal of the education authorities to make a sufficiently clear distinction between children with global and specific learning difficulties. Learning support teachers found themselves positioned uncomfortably between parents and education authorities, accepting the continuum view of learning difficulties but believing that children with specific learning difficulties needed more intensive and specialized tuition than could be provided by support in the mainstream class.

Finch (1984) has suggested that researchers have not only a responsibility to report honestly their findings but also to offer an interpretation which will seek to ensure that they are not used in a manner which might be damaging to already disadvantaged groups. She offers, as an example, her work on playgroups, which indicated that those in working-class areas were generally run less well than those in middle-class areas, leading, on occasion, to potentially dangerous situations. Until she had developed an interpretation of her findings which avoided the promotion of a deficit view of working-class mothers, Finch did not publish her work. In the same way, in our report to the SOED and in subsequent papers (Riddell, Brown and Duffield, 1994a; 1994b), we endeavoured to make sense of the gulf between education authority and parental perspectives. For instance, we explored the significance of the fact that our sample of parents was predominantly middle class and had a clear notion of how to use the system in order to gain preferential resourcing for their children. In the context of waning education authority control and the promotion of parent power, we pointed out how a group like this might succeed in its goals at the expense of others who lacked similar cultural resources and organizational backup. By offering such a commentary, we hoped that our data would not be used to uphold the claims of the dyslexia lobby and undermine the efforts of education authorities to attend to the needs of all children in distributing resources. This seemed to us to be particularly important in the context of devolved school management which, although not in place in Scotland at the time of the research, appeared likely to intensify competition for funding.

RESPONSE TO THE RESEARCH

One of the difficulties of undertaking policy-orientated research is that, inevitably, once the work is in the public domain, the researchers are no longer able to exercise control over how it will be read. Since the publication of the final report we have disseminated our findings in a number of ways, producing an accessible summary in the Scottish Office Interchange series, organizing a conference for voluntary organizations and local authority policy-makers and speaking to small groups of psychologists, voluntary organizations and other interested groups such as SKILL (the organization for disabled students in further and higher education). Given our interpretation of the parents' perspective, we suspected that the Dyslexia Association might reject the research. On the contrary, in a letter to the Scottish Minister for Education the Secretary of the Scottish Dyslexia Association indicated satisfaction with the conduct of the research and the dissemination conference, but depression at the findings.

She commented: 'We are dismayed by the indicators of political influence by those in positions of educational responsibility and the negative effect it has on those people working in the "field". Bureaucracy is becoming too powerful and is often not working to the benefit of the child.' According to the Scottish Dyslexia Association, the research revealed a portrait of psychological services '. . . in a state of shambles, indoctrinated by an attitude totally alien to reality' and a learning support service which '. . . wastes a great deal of valuable time in their method of operation, i.e. classroom observation, acting as a consultant with the class teacher. This could be readjusted in order to allow more time spent on specific help to the child'. This was an account of the research which we certainly did not recognize.

The Dyslexia Institute, on the other hand, took great exception to some of the comments made by education authority personnel. Following the publication of the report, we received a letter from them referring to their 'great distress' at its contents. In their view, many of the comments were '. . . inaccurate, grossly misinterpreting the nature and scope of the Dyslexia Institute's work and made largely without consultation with Dyslexia Institute staff'. Our response was that we were certainly not endorsing but presenting the views of educational psychologists, some of whom did undoubtedly hold negative views of the Dyslexia Institute and its work.

In terms of gauging the Scottish Office response, little has been received in terms of official feedback. However, we heard recently that a decision had been made to take over the funding of a specific learning difficulties development post at a college of education which had been funded initially by the Scottish Dyslexia

Trust, a charity supported by businesses and individuals. The aim is to develop teaching materials on specific learning difficulties at undergraduate and post-graduate levels and distance-learning packages. Although not wishing to criticize the work of the person in post, we commented critically on the general principle that voluntary bodies should be able to buy a share in the teacher education curriculum. The development project on specific learning difficulties is very likely to boost teacher awareness in this area, but this may be at the expense of groups such as those with moderate learning difficulties or social, emotional and behavioural difficulties, who do not have the backing of wealthy advocacy groups to support their claims for priority treatment. A further development which has taken place since the end of the project concerns an adjustment of terminology in the latest Scottish Office publication on special needs and the 5–14 programme (SOED, 1993). Whereas previously the term 'specific learning difficulties' had been used in all official government publications, '. . . providing special programmes in reading and writing for pupils with dyslexia' (p. 22) is now listed as a key role for specialist learning support staff. Overall, we feel that the initiatives which have developed since the publication of our research findings do not reflect the key points emerging from our research.

CONCLUSION

In this chapter we have tried to provide an overview of our initial decision to undertake a policy-focused piece of research on specific learning difficulties for the SOED. We outlined the debate which surrounds government-sponsored educational research in Scotland, with some critics claiming that it almost inevitably produces poor-quality research which is used to justify decisions which have already been reached. We offered our defence of policy-orientated research, partly on the grounds that all funded research is likely to be connected in some way with policy, a trend set to continue in the future with the government's emphasis on the contribution of social research to wealth creation (Duchy of Lancaster, 1993). More importantly, we agreed with Finch's argument that it is almost inconceivable for social researchers to be able to operate in a policy-free environment. What is needed is a clear understanding of the policy issues involved, the interest groups competing for a stake in the research, the significance of the methods employed and the importance of a sensitive interpretation of findings.

In the case of our research into specific learning difficulties, we were aware that this was an area which threw up major challenges to the post-Warnock conceptualization of special educational needs. In contrast with the greater emphasis on the social construction of learning difficulties following the Warnock Report, the Dyslexia Association and other voluntary organizations clearly wished to tip the balance back towards a child-deficit notion of learning difficulties and the categorization of those with special educational needs as a means of establishing funding priorities.

Our research strategy involved elucidating the significance of particular conceptualizations of specific learning difficulties for policy and practice. The research methods we chose were deliberately not so much geared to the illumination of individual experience as to the implications of particular constructions of specific learning difficulties for policy. We endeavoured to present the perspectives of a wide range of interest groups in terms which they could recognize, but ultimately offered our interpretation, thus using what might be criticized as an authoritative researcher voice. We did this consciously and without apology, since we believe that it is the responsibility of the researcher not simply to describe but also to offer some sort of analysis and interpretation, making clear that others may wish to draw alternative conclusions and presenting sufficient data to allow them to do this. Our general conclusion was that in the area of special needs the emphasis on consumer choice was in danger of tilting the balance of power too far towards predominantly middle-class groups such as parents of children with specific learning difficulties, skewing resources away from other groups such as children with moderate learning difficulties or social, emotional and behavioural difficulties who are predominantly working class in their family of origin and who are not well supported by charities and advocacy groups.

Although our goal was to retain an agnostic stance with regard to the nature and origins of specific learning difficulties, this did not mean that we were claiming that our position was value free. As we explained at the start of this chapter, we had a commitment to the wider group of children with special educational needs, whom we recognized were socially and economically disadvantaged. We felt that, as discussed earlier, the Dyslexia Association construction of specific learning difficulties was potentially damaging to this wider group, but this did not imply that we lacked sympathy for individual children with specific learning difficulties and their families, for whom few would claim resources are adequate.

What effect did our determination to problematize learning difficulties have on the research? We were aware of the great effort involved in sustaining a critical stance throughout, particularly given the extreme helpfulness of the voluntary organizations and parents compared with the more frosty approach of some of the education authorities. However, the unease expressed by some professionals with regard to the categorization of children, although a complicating factor in the research, served as a useful reminder that neat terminology should not be used to gloss over conceptual uncertainty. When we talked and spoke about children with specific learning difficulties, we tried to remind ourselves that what we really meant was children defined by some as experiencing specific learning difficulties.

Finally, it is important to consider our feelings at the end of the project. Preliminary indications suggest that the research may have been interpreted by the Scottish Office as indicating the need for greater concentration on children with specific learning difficulties in teacher education courses and on individual tuition of such children in school. The adoption of the term 'dyslexia' in recent policy statements, with its connotations of a child-deficit notion of learning difficulties and its implicit assumption of separate categories of special educational needs, also indicates a retreat from some fundamental aspects of the Warnock Report. To some extent this serves to reinforce a central point made by the research, that the way in which learning difficulties are understood is crucial in terms of the actions which then follow, including the distribution of resources. We hoped that documenting this struggle would be helpful for those who were trying to defend the wider interests of children with special educational needs and of course we may have been successful in achieving this goal. However, the possibility that our findings might be used to support policies which clash with our own values is worrying and underlines the inherent dangers of policy-focused research.

REFERENCES

Abberley, P. (1987) 'The concept of oppression and the development of a social theory of disability', *Disability, Handicap and Society*, Vol. 2, no. 1, pp. 5–19.

Auger, J. (1990) School Boards' Pack. British Dyslexia Association, London.

Barnes, C. (1991) *Disabled People in Britain and Discrimination: A Case for Anti-Discrimination Legislation*. Hurst & Co., London.

Bell, C. and Newby, H. (eds) (1977) *Doing Sociological Research*. Allen & Unwin, London.

British Dyslexia Association (undated) *Dyslexia: The Hidden Handicap*. British Dyslexia Association, London.

Brown, S. (1993) 'Changes in higher education: changes for research.' Opening lecture to the Annual Conference of the Scottish Educational Research Association, St Andrews University, 30 September.

Department of Education and Science (1978) *Special Educational Needs* (Warnock Report). HMSO, London.

Duchy of Lancaster (1993) *Realising our Potential: A Strategy for Science, Engineering and Technology*. HMSO, London.

Finch, J. (1984) 'It's great to have someone to talk to: the ethics and politics of interviewing women', in C. Bell and H. Roberts (eds) *Social Researching: Politics, Problems, Practice*. Routledge & Kegan Paul, London.

Finch, J. (1986) *Research and Policy: The Uses of Qualitative Methods in Social and Educational Research*. Falmer Press, London.

Fulcher, G. (1989) *Disabling Policies? A Comparative Approach to Education Policy and Disability*. Falmer Press, London.

Heward, C. and Lloyd-Smith, M. (1991) 'Assessing the impact of legislation on special educational needs – an historical analysis', *Journal of Education Policy*, Vol. 5, no. 1, pp. 21–36.

Humes, W. (1986) *The Ruling Class in Scottish Education*. Scottish Academic Press, Edinburgh.

Jayaratne, T. E. (1983) 'The value of quantitative methodology for feminist research', in G. Bowles and R. Duelli Klein (eds) *Theories of Women's Studies*. Routledge, London.

Lather, P. (1991) *Getting Smart: Feminist Research and Pedagogy With/in the Post-Modern*. Routledge, New York.

Oakley, A. (1981) 'Interviewing women: a contradiction in terms', in H. Roberts (ed.) *Doing Feminist Research*. Routledge & Kegan Paul, London.

Oliver, M. (1988) 'The social and political context of educational policy: the case of special needs', in L. Barton (ed.) *The Politics of Special Educational Needs*. Falmer Press, London.

Oliver, M. (1990) *The Politics of Disablement*. Macmillan, London.

Pumfrey, P. and Reason, R. (1991) *Specific Learning Difficulties: Dyslexia: Challenges and Responses*. NFER-Nelson, Windsor.

Riddell, S. I. (1989) 'Exploiting the exploited? The ethics of feminist educational research', in R. G. Burgess (ed.) *The Ethics of Educational Research*. Falmer Press, London.

Riddell, S. I., Brown, S. and Duffield, J. (forthcoming) 'Conflicts of policies and models: the case of specific learning difficulties', in S. Riddell and S. Brown (eds) *Special Educational Needs Policy in the 1990s: Warnock in the Market Place*. Routledge, London.

Riddell, S. I., Brown, S. and Duffield, J. (forthcoming) 'Parental power and special educational needs: the case of specific learning difficulties', *British Educational Research Journal* (special issue on special needs, integration and entitlement).

Riddell, S. I., Duffield, J., Brown, S. and Ogilvy, C. (1992) *Specific Learning Difficulties: Policy, Practice and Provision* (Report to the Scottish Office Education Department). Department of Education, University of Stirling.

Scott, S. (1984) 'The personable and the powerful: gender and status in sociological research', in C. Bell and D. Roberts (eds) *Social Researching: Politics, Problems, Practice*. Routledge & Kegan Paul, London.

Scottish Education Department (1978) *The Education of Pupils with Learning Difficulties in Primary and Secondary Schools in Scotland: A Progress Report by HM Inspectors of Schools*. HMSO, Edinburgh.

Scottish Office Education Department (1993) *Support for Learning Special Educational Needs within the 5–14 Curriculum: Staff Development Materials Part One: Sharing Ideas*. SOED, Edinburgh.

Townsend, P. (1979) *Poverty in the United Kingdom*. Penguin Books, Harmondsworth.

Troyna, B. and Carrington, B. (1989) 'Whose side are we on? Ethical dilemmas in research on "race" and education', in R. G. Burgess (ed.) *The Ethics of Educational Research*. Falmer Press, London.

Walker, A. (1982) *Unqualified and Underemployed: Handicapped Young People in the Labour Market*. Macmillan, London.

4

RISK, ROUTINE AND REWARD: CONFRONTING PERSONAL AND SOCIAL CONSTRUCTS IN RESEARCH ON SPECIAL EDUCATIONAL NEEDS

Hazel Bines

Research on special educational needs can be one of the most difficult and demanding aspects of educational and other social research. The researcher must confront a range of issues and dilemmas, together with many personal and social values and vested interests. In addition, past and current research on special educational needs has tended to take constructs of needs and systems of provision for granted. Although there are now some more critical perspectives, largely based on sociological theories and methods, there is still insufficient analysis of many aspects of policy and provision. It is therefore hard to ensure that research on special educational needs does not simply confirm existing beliefs and systems but rather contributes to critique and change.

Research also requires particular knowledge, skills and experience and can be difficult to implement. This may have an effect on research outcomes. The use of particular methods may mean that certain beliefs and actions are not explored or that the validity of the perspectives of those being researched is neglected or denied. Inappropriate explanations and theories may undermine the development of approaches which articulate issues of practice with wider social critique and which evaluate accounts of particular individuals and situations with questions about the social construction of needs or the impact of social systems. The researcher may also have hidden or explicit values which make it difficult to be truly critical, particularly if he or she comes from a background of professional work in the area and thus has vested interests in particular approaches. In turn, research concerning the views of others working in a professional capacity may be subject to such interests on their part, which may make it difficult to operationalize because of a lack of common understanding or feelings of threat and resistance. Research may therefore slip back into traditional constructs and paradigms despite the researcher's original critical intentions. It may also create or legitimate definitions of needs, policies and approaches which are just as damaging as those which the research has investigated and criticized.

Research on special educational needs is also largely concerned with children and young people, who have a marginal voice in society in any case, let alone if they are considered to have special needs. It can thus be difficult to recognize the importance of the perspectives of those labelled 'special'. Self-advocacy by young people and adults, and research which gives those considered to have special needs a voice, are beginning to redress such problems. However, there is still a need to recognize more fully the ethical, theoretical and methodological questions involved in researchers, rather than the researched, having the dominant say.

The expectations and processes involved in doing research can therefore be as problematic as the nature of the research itself. Reflective critique thus requires careful examination of personal and social constructs of both special educational needs and research. Both these aspects will now be explored in relation to some of my research during the last decade – namely, research carried out some years ago on the development of new approaches to special educational needs provision in secondary schools and my current research on the developing roles of LEAs and schools in the new framework established by recent legislation. I will also consider the particular issues faced by experienced practitioners moving into research as inexperienced researchers, together with some more general arguments about research, drawing on particular aspects and experience of research on special educational needs.

VALUES, BELIEFS AND RESEARCH

The constructs held by individuals are likely to involve a mixture of political, ethical and theoretical ideas which have been shaped by particular knowledge, values and experience and by membership of particular social groups. These then interact with research in a number of different ways. Although the processes involved in doing educational research have become more widely documented (Burgess, 1984; 1985a; 1985b; 1985c; Walford, 1987; 1991), little attention has been given to this aspect. However it is important to consider how personal values and beliefs may shape the research topic, methods and outcomes. For example, my interest in doing research on special educational needs is linked to a long-standing political and ethical commitment to a society based on equality and diversity rather than prejudice and disadvantage. Although I have chosen to draw on sociological perspectives because I consider they are particularly appropriate, this may be due in part to my affinity with sociology as a result of my undergraduate studies. My experience as a teacher has also been very influential in that teaching, rather than family or significant social experience, has been the main context within which I have developed my knowledge of special educational needs. I have spent a number of years teaching children and young people considered to have learning and behaviour difficulties and have a number of strong views about the importance of educational opportunities, the effectiveness of integration and of the right teaching approaches and the interesting and rewarding nature (most of the time!) of teaching such pupils. This has undoubtedly influenced my research, which has concentrated on professional issues rather than other aspects of special educational needs such as the perspectives of parents.

The merging of such a background with the theories and processes of research requires some critical examination. For example, although I have found that sociological perspectives on special educational needs are congruent with many of my beliefs and values, they remain both difficult and challenging. Certainly I support the view that traditional paradigms have had a number of problematic consequences for children, young people and adults considered to have special educational needs and have resulted in needs being centred on the individual and his or her supposed deficits rather than the social beliefs and systems which may have created such needs in the first place (Barton and Tomlinson, 1981a). I also agree that power and control are key issues in critical analysis, that current approaches to policy and practice legitimate and support a range of professional and other social interests and that those considered to have special educational needs are wrongly segregated and excluded from many of the educational and social opportunities and experiences available to others (Tomlinson, 1982; Barton and Tomlinson, 1981b; 1984; Barton, 1988; 1989; Oliver, 1990).

However, translating such perspectives into my research has raised a number of issues. Although I believe that most special educational needs are socially constructed, and that even those with an apparently non-social cause, such as physical impairment, may also be grounded in society's willingness, or otherwise, to develop appropriate health and technological investment, it can be difficult to maintain such social perspectives under the day-to-day pressures of teaching and research. I have also found it hard to resolve the dilemma between providing specialist help which may reinforce particular constructions of need and developing an inclusive approach which may, however, result in some needs being neglected in the current system of education. At the time when I started my research on provision in secondary schools, there was also very little research on the curriculum and I therefore drew heavily on my professional views, most of which were framed in terms of traditional approaches to what was then termed remedial provision. Professional experience and culture has also made it difficult to agree with all of the sociological criticisms of professional vested interests, even though I am aware that policy and provision for special educational needs are often neglected and marginalized and that certain professional attitudes and practices need to be confronted.

Values and beliefs are also subject to change. My research experience generated a strong interest in the issues involved in developing curricular and whole-school approaches to special educational needs. I now feel that we should give much more research attention to the curriculum, particularly since the implementation of the National Curriculum, and that the argument that special educational needs can be a touchstone for evaluating and developing the education of all children and young people (Clough and Thompson, 1987) is very important in terms of generating improvements and change. I have also become concerned that, despite its apparent critical and reflexive potential, sociological study of education has tended to reflect the general marginalization of special educational needs. Some of my work has therefore concentrated on arguing that special educational provision is a crucial and valuable area of sociological inquiry. Although this has not altered my primary commitment to the issues of practice, my view of the research agenda is now much wider. Such perspectives have also been shaped by my move into teacher and higher education, which has both required and provided more opportunities for the development of a broader approach. Consideration therefore also needs to be given to the ways in which new roles, as well as new knowledge and experience, may be important factors in changes in values and beliefs.

I would also like to see a much more open engagement with political and personal values so that the assumptions underlying research are made clear. However, that requires an acknowledgement that the process of doing research, and personal constructs of research, may be as important as the nature of the research itself and may shape research outcomes in a number of ways. This will now be illustrated in relation to my own research experiences.

PERSONAL AND SOCIAL CONSTRUCTS OF RESEARCH

As suggested earlier in this chapter, research can be demanding and difficult. Taking up a research role from a background of practice can therefore be particularly challenging. Managing research alongside professional responsibilities involves coping with two identities and two forms of work, as well as the many pressures on time and energy. Although the opportunity to do full-time research may seem more inviting, it also has many problems, not least the change to a different professional identity and a different way of life that is very unfamiliar. As I exchanged the role of a special educational needs co-ordinator in a secondary school for full-time research for a PhD I developed a number of metaphors and analogies to cope with the stresses involved. I found it particularly helpful to draw on other potentially difficult and risky ventures I had undertaken as a mountaineer. I therefore conceptualized this particular research experience as a mountain journey. Although I had started with some grasp of landscape and direction, and some knowledge and experience in the rucksack, the rest was uncharted territory. Later on I felt as if I were submerged in avalanches of data and had to find my way through the mists of uncertainty as to theory and methodology. I also had a number of regular encounters with the bogs of tedium and despondency and the precipices of ethics and commitment. However, my knowledge that such problems were characteristic of such journeys, and had been overcome in the past, did help to sustain both confidence and perseverance.

Nevertheless, the research remained both difficult and challenging. I had to learn about the techniques of research and make myself familiar with a range of literature. The reading was as hard as a steep uphill climb in mountaineering and, although I assumed that the intellectual equivalent of physical fitness would gradually develop, this was little comfort in the first few weeks as I struggled to read what I considered to be some extremely difficult ideas! I also found it very hard to enter staffrooms in unfamiliar schools as a researcher. This change in identity was one of the most problematic aspects of the research process and I often wished I could take on the more familiar and secure mantle of being a teacher.

As I began to implement the research and collected a range of extremely interesting data, I felt happier with the research role. However, I soon realized how hard it can be to analyse such data. I had chosen to base much of my research on interviews with teachers and therefore had many pages of transcripts. The first problem therefore centred on grasping the full extent of data which I had collected. I then had to identify analyses and explanations which seemed most appropriate and which also reflected the theoretical orientations I wished to pursue. Although I would judge the outcome as worth while, it was undoubtedly affected by the intellectual and organizational difficulties involved. The uncertainty and anxiety as to whether I would complete this process successfully were also very challenging. Above all, I found that doing research was often, like mountaineering, a lonely activity. Even though there may be companionship and support, each individual has to confront and come to terms with the task, and the fears, alone.

Although I am now more experienced in research, I still have similar problems. This is partly because research is difficult, even for the more experienced researcher. However it is also due to the research equivalent of extending one's mountaineering horizons and seeking yet harder and harder challenges. I am now very aware of the range of research which needs to be done and the importance of making some contribution. However I must also admit that I enjoy research and the satisfaction of overcoming difficulties. I have therefore been forced to recognize that I undertake research not only because of my political and social commitment but also because of its rewarding intellectual challenge. Nevertheless I also consider it to be a difficult and risky activity, which can lead to a tendency to play safe to the detriment of critical theory. Personal constructs of research, and the complex mix of personal and social drives involved, may thus be as important as personal and social constructs of the area being researched. Although I believe that research is a valuable social activity, it does have a number of personal dimensions which are not always acknowledged, many of which centre on the issues of risk, routine and reward.

RISK, ROUTINE AND REWARDS IN RESEARCH

Although my comparison of research with mountaineering is a personal construct, I would argue that it has some general import. This is because mountaineering has developed an explicit culture of risk, routine and reward which can be used to crystallize and examine such issues. A commonality of experience can be drawn, even though this may not be apparent at first. For example, although risk is most evident in terms of potentially physically dangerous activities such as mountaineering, it is also highly relevant to research. As Mike Thompson, anthropologist and mountaineer, has noted, anyone who sets out to provide an explanation for something where previous attempts have failed, or who questions the validity of an explanation which most people feel is perfectly adequate, is taking an intellectual risk (Thompson, 1983).

There are also the same tensions between subjective factors, such as expertise, experience, commitment and judgement, and the objective conditions and problems which may be encountered. However, whereas the mountaineer engages with weather, loose rock or crevassed ice, the researcher is concerned with the natural or social phenomena being studied. The outcome of the enterprise will then depend in part on the nature of such conditions or phenomena and in part on the capacity of the researcher or mountaineer. For the latter, risk and success are largely determined by the balance between the subjective and the objective. Risk increases when subjective factors are not sufficient for the task in hand and/or objective conditions are extreme and highly unpredictable. An imbalance, or an extreme undertaking, may lead to discomfort, danger or even death. For the researcher there are similar tensions between objective factors and subjective capacity. The subsequent risks may be less obvious, but nevertheless exist, given that an unsuccessful outcome may lead to loss of credibility, wasted time and intellectual investment and the potential spoiling of a research career.

It would therefore seem that a key priority is to reduce risk. However, both mountaineering and research have an aesthetic and ethics of risk. For the mountaineer, the aesthetic lies in finding the hardest, cleanest and most attractive route possible and/or altering the balance between subjective and objective factors, the latter allowing those who are less capable or experienced also to participate by trying something which may be easy for others but difficult for them. Ethics are then based on pursuing this aesthetic as well as certain ground rules which apply to all, such as not using particular equipment or tactics on particular routes (Tejada-Flores, 1978; Thompson, 1983). The aesthetic in research is concerned with tackling central, difficult and exciting research problems with innovative methodologies to achieve maximum empirical and theoretical outcomes. Ethics are concerned with the pursuit of this aesthetic together with issues such as appropriate methodology, not cooking the results, acknowledging other people's work and, sometimes, the impact on the researched or society as a whole. For many types of research, unlike mountaineering, there is also the ethic of conducting a socially useful activity and for both there is the reward of overcoming the challenges of, and working within, demanding aesthetic and ethical frameworks.

Both research and mountaineering are also grounded in routine. Moreover, this routine may not be apparent to those who are not involved and who see both activities as being exciting and different from the demands of ordinary life, even though they generate hard work, difficult conditions and isolation. These are not always recognized as common and inevitable aspects of either activity, leading those involved, particularly for the first time, to think that there must be something wrong with their approach. Both also involve a high level of personal commitment, anxiety and fear, even though this may be quickly forgotten once the objective is achieved. Nevertheless, a willingness to face up to such problems, as well as routine demands, remains one of the conditions of success.

These issues of risk, routine and rewards need more consideration in relation to research. For example, it could be argued that the lack of critical approaches comes in part from the reluctance of researchers working in special educational needs, or indeed other areas, to recognize or confront the risk of challenging traditional constructs and paradigms or engaging in new and difficult work. For research, unlike mountaineering, there is an added dimension, namely, that the researcher is inevitably part of the phenomenon being studied and will construct further phenomena as a consequence of his or her research. Those who are being researched are thus also put at risk, since they will be subject to the researcher's beliefs, actions and products. If the research is appropriately and effectively conducted, there may be mutual benefits for both the researcher and the researched. However, if there are difficulties and problems, the outcome may be very different. Whereas the researcher may escape relatively unscathed, and indeed may emerge with accolades from fellow researchers, those being researched may be the victims of misinterpretation and stereotyping, sudden and unwelcome public interest and, above all, the policies which are consequently, and inappropriately, developed.

Both aesthetics and ethics have value in that they set high standards for process and outcomes and ensure that difficult problems will be investigated. At the same time, they tend to suggest that the routine is unexciting, even though it is an inevitable component. Painstaking and long-term research, or the difficult process of generating formal theory, may be avoided in favour of the study of new and exciting substantive areas. Such trends can be problematic. As Quicke (1986) has noted, sociological studies of deviancy have focused on the more 'exotic' types of pupil life and behaviour rather than what might be seen as somewhat mundane learning or other difficulties. The sense of adventure and risk associated with, for example, research on rebellious male youth, may lead to neglect of those whose lives appear routine and uninteresting, even though both social and research ethics would normally make them a priority. In addition, the emergence of particular research topics as crucial and thus highly rewarding challenges may lead to neglect of equally important examples elsewhere. Studies of power and inequity have concentrated on class, gender and race and on mainstream schooling rather than on disability or special education (Barton and Oliver, 1992). Despite the argument that special educational needs and special education can provide particularly illuminating examples of sociological issues in curriculum and policy change (Bines, 1993), they still remain neglected for this purpose. The routine and apparently unrewarding nature of certain research has therefore had an effect in relation to the development of research on special educational needs and its centrality to the research agenda.

There are of course many good reasons for the above problems, including external pressures on the research community to develop selective profiles of research excellence to secure funding, general cuts in resources for research, the capacity of certain research areas rather than others to attract funding and general social notions of research. The marginality of special educational needs and provision is also bound to be reflected in the relationship of research on this area to other educational research. However, it needs to be recognized that research, including research on special educational needs, is itself a social construction, subject to individual and systemic beliefs, interactions and pressures. My own research will now be discussed in this light.

RESEARCH ON SPECIAL NEEDS IN SECONDARY SCHOOLS

I started my research in 1983 as a full-time PhD student, after 12 years of teaching in primary, secondary and special schools and services. My last post was as head of what was then called 'remedial education', in a medium-sized comprehensive school in South Yorkshire. Appointed to develop the new advisory cross-curricular role of remedial teachers/special needs co-ordinators (Galletley, 1976; McNicholas, 1979; Lewis, 1984; NARE, 1979; 1985), I did not find it easy to implement this new approach and encountered a range of problems, including my own lack of expertise across the whole curriculum, teacher resistance to models of in-class support rather than segregation and dilemmas of resource allocation between individual pupils and general curriculum development and change. At the time it was being suggested that the model was highly effective and only needed appropriate expertise to make it work. Although my situation did eventually develop more positively, I felt there was insufficient awareness of the difficulties of implementing this model and had some major concerns about its value for both teachers and pupils. I thus decided to undertake full-time research to allow me to undertake case studies in secondary schools other than my own.

The element of risk in terms of personal investment was therefore quite high in that I gave up my job and would be living on a grant rather than a salary for three years at an institution some distance from home. However the major risk, which I had to confront very quickly, involved my potential capacity to do sustained research. The aesthetic of research was very strong in that I wanted the research to be of value and to succeed at the best level possible for me. At this stage, however, there was an imbalance between subjective factors such as expertise and experience and the objective problems of the research, promising a high degree of discomfort at best and, at worst, the unrewarding possibility of the research equivalent of a major mountain expedition retreat.

This imbalance undoubtedly had an effect on the research. As noted earlier, although I felt that sociological perspectives were appropriate, I lacked confidence in both my theoretical and empirical knowledge. I therefore found it difficult to apply such perspectives to my research in ways which were fully effective. The research was also influenced by my particular definition of the social value of my research. Although I was undoubtedly pursuing some personal fulfilment, my major concern was to investigate the value of this new model for teachers and pupils, and thus help others who might have encountered some or all the difficulties that I had experienced. However, this professional orientation led to a somewhat exclusive focus on the needs and perspectives of teachers rather than pupils and on certain issues of practice rather than broader sociological critique. I started from the concerns of my own practice, that is, the perspective of the teacher rather than the pupil and, although I considered the implications for pupils, they were not central to the research design, which largely comprised interviews with special needs and subject teachers. In particular, I found it difficult to balance the perspectives of teachers and the constraints upon them with the implications of some of their beliefs and actions for pupils. Thus although I could appreciate why support in the classroom was perceived as much in terms of benefits to teachers as to pupils, given the isolation of classroom teaching and pressures of lack of expertise, workload and other stresses (Bines, 1986; 1987), I should have developed a more challenging critique in relation to benefits for pupils, and the ways in which some professional attitudes and practices can undermine pupils' learning experiences and achievements.

As the research developed I became very interested in potential conflicts between remedial or special needs teachers and subject and class teachers, in terms of support in the classroom and advice and other help on curriculum development and teaching methods. Such conflicts were apparent, and were explained in terms of subject and other professional territories and boundaries (Bines, 1986; 1987). This particular approach was reinforced by other work on curriculum change which had identified subject differences (e.g. Ball, 1981) and the then new but growing literature on subject subcultures and subject communities and their involvement in, and impact on, curricular change (e.g. Goodson, 1983; Goodson and Ball, 1984; Cooper, 1985). I took the opportunity to attach my work to what I regarded as a particularly aesthetically strong strand of educational research, in the sense discussed earlier. Although I feel this was the right decision, in that the research was immediately far more theoretically informed, such a focus inevitably drew me further into the perspectives and concerns of professionals rather than pupils, and into taking systems for given as I explored how they worked. It is my view that my research therefore contributed to, as well as explaining, the social construction of special educational needs by the professionals involved and failed to be sufficiently critical of systems.

The research therefore took certain constructs for granted and reinforced others. For example, by prioritizing the views of professionals, it maintained the belief that professional definitions of need and provision are more significant than those of pupils and parents. It also reinforced the notion that special needs teachers require a different expertise from other teachers by focusing on conflicts rather than commonalities of perspectives. Although such conflict was evident, the support it gave to my theory of subject communities became more important than the possibility that I was creating new explanations which would continue to polarize special and other educational provision.

However I do feel I did make one contribution to more critical explanations of constructs of special educational needs. As part of the research I explored subject teachers' perceptions of learning difficulties and was able to demonstrate that learning difficulties may have as much to do with the cognitive and pedagogical demands of different subjects, and the general constraints of teaching, as with any individual learning problems presented by pupils (Bines, 1986; 1987). This knowledge was challenging to my own constructs at first, given that these were based on a somewhat individualized notion of learning difficulties, but has since informed my teaching on special educational needs in teacher education and some of my subsequent writing. My more critical concerns in relation to professional attitudes and beliefs, including the lack of commitment to equal opportunities, have also been developed in subsequent work (e.g. Bines, 1988; Roaf and Bines, 1989). In terms of the ethic of producing socially critical and useful research, I feel I have therefore met some of the criteria I originally set myself.

The failure to produce a fully critical and articulated social and sociological account of special educational needs provision in secondary schools is an example of the gap between subjective capacity and objective conditions described earlier in this chapter. My commitment was high but my expertise and experience in research were limited, which affected both my performance and my judgement. I erred towards the perceptions of the professional, partly because I could not see I was doing this and partly because I felt slightly safer there. I also had strong feelings, as a teacher, about the demands and constraints of teaching. The tendency for the inexperienced (and experienced) researcher to 'go native' was reinforced by personal involvement in teacher culture and the view that some educational research had been too quick to identify teachers as culpable for continuing social and educational inequalities. Given some of the derision that teachers have recently experienced at the hands of a government intent on making a crisis of professional beliefs and action to justify its own reform agenda (Ball, 1990), it would seem to me that such a stance has some theoretical and ethical justification. It also led me to unpack the notion of professional interests in ways which I felt gave greater credence to the motivations of, and constraints on, professionals. At the time, given the work of Tomlinson and others, this felt like a very risky aspect of the research which might have problematic repercussions. I am pleased that I maintained this commitment to a potentially difficult line of research and that I continued to engage with the routine worries and concerns of practitioners in the field.

However I do recognize that I was also very concerned with the risks of the pragmatic operationalization of the research, in that if I asked teachers questions that were too challenging or threatening I might not get sufficient data. Although I would still believe that is the job of the researcher to ensure that the views of the researched, including professionals, are given validity and credence, I do now regret that some professional beliefs and actions were not treated critically enough. It seems to me that pupils, in the schools I researched and in general, were the unwitting participants in the risks of my research and that, for them, this particular enterprise was not very rewarding. They remained unacknowledged risk-takers, whom I did not fully consider. And although the marginalization of pupils, and others deemed to have special educational needs, is a society-wide issue that is not easily changed by individuals, it must be seen as an individual responsibility, just as I should more often remember the contribution of my particular feet to the erosion of our hills and the impact of my personal tourism and travel on some of the beautiful and remote landscapes and cultures of the Himalayas.

RESEARCH ON CURRENT POLICIES FOR SPECIAL EDUCATIONAL NEEDS

Evaluation of this earlier research shows how personal and social constructs of both research and special educational needs interact with the research process and affect both the focus and outcome of research. Some of this may be ascribed to inexperience. However, my continuing involvement in research suggests that such issues remain central. Issues of risk, routine and reward continue to be powerful aspects of the research process. Although my research provided a route into higher education, the opportunities since to do research have been extremely limited because of the pressures of my current post in teacher education. The risks of investing in problematic research, and the problems of managing the daily routine of research among other work, are considerable. Personal constructs of the key issues in research also remain influential.

My recent involvement in a collaborative research project on special educational needs with Oxfordshire LEA has offered a unique opportunity to consider the changing role of LEAs and schools in the light of the Code of Practice and other recent legislation and the development of new models of working suggested by HMI and the Audit Commission. Following devolution of many former LEA managerial responsibilities to schools, concern about the processes and outcomes of statementing and the continuing permeation of public services with quasi-market mechanisms, it is now being suggested that schools as contractors to LEAs should be given full responsibilities for providing for special educational needs and should be accountable for pupils' achievements and the deployment of resources allocated. Schools should also have succinct policies based on clear principles to increase their capability to provide for pupils with special educational needs, and should develop strategies to achieve objectives which can then be monitored and evaluated by themselves and external bodies (Audit Commission/HMI, 1992a; 1992b). The Code of Practice for special educational needs which has now been introduced (Department for Education, 1994) has reinforced such accountability, through a series of stages of assessment and intervention, individual education plans, regular monitoring and review and time limits for the making of statements of special needs. It will have considerable impact on the planning of curricular provision, the management of special educational needs in schools, the involvement of parents and the relationships between schools and LEAs. It therefore represents a substantial focus on, and change in, policy for special educational needs, in contrast to previous neglect of special educational needs in recent educational reforms.

Such developments offer a particular opportunity to research changing policy on special educational needs. However, such changes will have to take place within the context established by the 1988 Education Reform Act and other legislation, drawing pupils with special educational needs into the new curriculum and assessment, and budgetary and market, frameworks (Bowe and Ball, 1992). Thus although policy requirements for special educational needs have some specific dimensions, there are increasing links with policy analysis of educational reform in general. Such links are particularly interesting to me given my commitment, as outlined earlier, to ensuring that policy and provision for special educational needs are seen as a central and valuable focus for sociological research. However, that commitment also raises a number of issues about the continuing interaction between my values and beliefs and the focus and potential outcomes of my research. Although I believe that research on policy is a major priority, I have to consider whether my choice of research has also been influenced by particular theoretical orientations and concerns. In choosing to undertake such policy research, I am creating a particular definition of the determinants of the lives of those considered to have special educational needs and those who work with them. There are equally powerful arguments for continuing to look closely at the micro-contexts of schooling, family and social experience. Indeed, it could be suggested that these are the contexts that are most important to those concerned, even if they do take place within wider policy and social frameworks.

The choice of this particular research topic also raises other questions. There has been considerable debate about the recent development of the sociology of education, including its current tendency to 'policy drift', that is, study of recent government and other policies rather than the sustained development of theory. Concern has also been expressed in relation to some of the evaluative criteria involved in such research (Dale, 1992; Power, 1992; Shilling, 1993). I would like to feel that my focus on policy reflects a commitment to understanding, and changing, the contexts of practice and the experience of children and young people considered to have special educational needs. However, it may also reflect my continued ambivalence about my capacity to cope with, and contribute to, formal sociological theory.

The focus on the views of professionals must also be considered. There has been considerable criticism of the role of LEAs, including their potential to set up bureaucratic systems which both create special needs and weaken schools' willingness to take responsibility (e.g. Thomas, 1992). At the same time, these tendencies have to be seen in the context of increasing central control of the education system and the potential of some quite creative responses by LEAs to the new policy climate (Bines and Thomas, 1994). Past experience has demonstrated that I can be ambivalent about professional vested interests. The acid test of policy, and my research, must be the outcomes for pupils deemed to have special educational needs. There is also the issue of taking current systems of categorization, provision and funding for granted, particularly when the research focus is primarily the nature of change rather than the reasons why such systems were established in the first place. In addition, the focus of the research is wider, which means it will involve more unwitting risk-takers than before. Moreover, because time for the research is limited, and some of it will involve documentary analysis and questionnaires rather than a large number of personal interviews, the potential for misinterpretation of others' perspectives and experiences is very high. A system-wide focus may also mean less engagement with specific constructions of special educational needs.

However it seems to me, at this moment at least, that a system-based research project does have as much potential for challenging social constructions as detailed case studies of the type I previously completed. There is less chance of 'going native' into one particular culture through close intimacy and more chance of seeing the wider repercussions of individual and institutional decision-making for children and young people with special educational needs as a whole. Whereas individual situations are amenable to a range of different interpretations, and thus may not be evaluated so critically, the exigencies and consequences of the system are both clear and challenging.

I am therefore fairly confident that this research is not an attempt to escape the routine and realities of everyday life in schools in favour of more adventurous policy analysis. Nevertheless, the interaction of my various values, beliefs, theories and experiences with this research must be a continuing focus of critique. The subjective factors of expertise, experience and judgement have improved since my earlier research experiences. At the same time, this research poses new objective difficulties which make it quite risky, such as the venture into the difficult and somewhat uncharted territory of marketization and public service restructuring. I also no longer have the excuse of inexperience in research. I suspect that although incipient middle age is tempering some of my mountaineering exploits, the aesthetic of challenge and risk remains in both my physical and intellectual enterprises. Although justified by academic and socially oriented motives, this research also fulfils my desire for risk and its associated rewards. At least I have learnt that other participants must be a priority and that if one is going to act in a risky way for oneself, one must be absolutely willing to recognize this and to face up to possible and actual consequences.

CONCLUSION

Thompson argues that there are those who tend towards risk-taking and those who tend towards risk avoidance. Risk-takers are also often fairly individualistic, although risk-sharing is another strategy (Thompson, 1983). Risk is, however, only a choice for some and there are far too many people, including many with special educational needs, who are put permanently at risk by our current system of education, social inequality and the lack of social justice. It would therefore seem to be axiomatic that those who are able should take the risks involved in research designed to challenge and change this situation and should be willing to confront the personal and social issues generated.

Nevertheless, the experience of research discussed in this chapter might lead one to conclude that research is therefore so laden with problems and demands that it is not worth while to begin, especially if one is not an experienced researcher who might be able to identify and overcome some of these issues. However, such defeatism is both unhelpful and unconstructive. First, it allows traditional paradigms to remain dominant. Secondly, it puts the issues of research before the needs of people, given there is a chance that some research, however flawed, may have beneficial outcomes. Thirdly, it fails to recognize that research is a difficult activity and part of the challenge is the confrontation of such problems. Finally, it avoids the question of how to improve research.

It seems to me that we need to take a more collective approach. First, we should recognize that the 'private troubles' of research are actually public issues, just as we have recognized that special educational needs have a social as well as an individual dimension. There could then be some collective risk-sharing, not to reduce the risks of research but rather to pool resources and ideas, including those which can be contributed by people with special educational needs themselves. Support would then be available for the problems of dealing with the risks, routine work and rewards involved in research. More open and reflective sharing of the ways in which personal and social constructs interact with research, as demonstrated in this book, would also identify the influence of such constructs, the ways they may create and legitimate certain perspectives and practices and the means to become more critical. We might then achieve a truly social and reflective approach to research on special educational needs which would reduce the risks for those who are the subject of such research and ensure that situational and system-wide inequities were more fully addressed. Certainly, whatever the personal dimensions and outcomes, the collective and social rewards of research should be the major aim.

ACKNOWLEDGEMENTS

I would like to acknowledge the help offered by Peter Clough and Len Barton through their comments on earlier drafts of this chapter.

REFERENCES

Audit Commission/HMI (1992a) *Getting in on the Act, Provision for Pupils with Special Needs: The National Picture*. HMSO, London.
Audit Commission/HMI (1992b) *Getting the Act Together, Provision for Pupils with Special Educational Needs, A Management Handbook for Schools and Local Education Authorities*. HMSO, London.
Ball, S. J. (1981) *Beachside Comprehensive*. Falmer Press, Lewes.
Ball, S. J. (1990) *Politics and Policy Making in Education*. Routledge, London.
Barton, L. (ed.) (1988) *The Politics of Special Educational Needs*. Falmer Press, Lewes.
Barton, L. (ed.) (1989) *Disability and Dependency*. Falmer Press, Lewes.
Barton, L. and Oliver, M. (1992) 'Special needs: personal trouble or private issue?', in M. Arnot and L. Barton (eds) *Voicing Concerns: Sociological Perspectives on Contemporary Education Reforms*. Triangle Books, Wallingford.
Barton, L. and Tomlinson, S. (1981a) 'Introduction', in L. Barton and S. Tomlinson (eds) *Special Education: Policy, Practices and Social Issues*. Harper & Row, London.
Barton, L. and Tomlinson, S. (eds) (1981b) *Special Education: Policy, Practices and Social Issues*. Harper & Row, London.
Barton, L. and Tomlinson, S. (eds) (1984) *Special Education and Social Interests*. Croom Helm, Beckenham.
Bines, H. (1986) *Redefining Remedial Education*. Croom Helm, Beckenham.
Bines, H. (1987) The redefinition of remedial education. Unpublished DPhil thesis, Department of Educational Studies, University of Oxford.

Bines, H. (1988) 'Equality, community and individualism: the development and implementation of the "whole school approach" to special educational needs', in L.
Barton (ed.) *The Politics of Special Educational Needs.* Falmer Press, Lewes.

Bines, H. (1993) 'Curriculum change: the case of special education', *British Journal of
Sociology of Education,* Vol. 14, no. 1, pp. 75–90.

Bines, H. and Thomas, G. (1994) 'From bureaucrats to advocates? The changing role
of LEAs', *Support for Learning,* Vol. 9, no. 2, pp. 61–7.

Bowe, R. and Ball, S. J. with Gold, A. (1992) *Reforming Education and Changing
Schools.* Routledge, London.

Burgess, R. G. (ed.) (1984) *The Research Process in Educational Settings: Ten Case
Studies.* Falmer Press, Lewes.

Burgess, R. G. (ed.) (1985a) *Field Methods in the Study of Education.* Falmer Press,
Lewes.

Burgess, R. G. (ed.) (1985b) *Strategies of Educational Research.* Falmer Press, Lewes.

Burgess, R. G. (ed.) (1985c) *Issues in Educational Research.* Falmer Press, Lewes.

Clough, P. and Thompson, D. (1987) 'Curricular approaches to learning difficulties:
problems for the paradigm', in B. Franklin (ed.) *Learning Disabilities: Dissenting
Essays.* Falmer Press, Lewes.

Cooper, B. (1985) *Renegotiating Secondary School Mathematics.* Falmer Press, Lewes.

Dale, R. (1992) 'Recovering from a Pyrrhic victory? Quality, relevance and impact in
the sociology of education', in M. Arnot and L. Barton (eds) *Voicing Concerns:
Sociological Perspectives on Contemporary Education Reforms.* Triangle Books,
Wallingford.

Department for Education (1994) *Code of Practice on the Identification and
Assessment of Special Educational Needs,* DFE, London.

Galletley, I. (1976) 'How to do away with yourself', *Remedial Education,* Vol. 11, no.
3, pp. 149–52.

Goodson, I. F. (1983) *School Subjects and Curriculum Change.* Croom Helm,
Beckenham.

Goodson, I. F. and Ball, S. J. (eds) (1984) *Defining the Curriculum: Histories and
Ethnographies.* Falmer Press, Lewes.

Lewis, G. (1984) 'A supportive role at secondary level', *Remedial Education,* Vol. 19,
no. 1, pp. 7–12.

NARE (1979) *Guidelines No. 2: The Role of Remedial Teachers.* NARE, Stafford.

NARE (1985) *Guidelines No. 6: Teaching Roles for Special Educational Needs.*
NARE, Stafford.

McNicholas, J. M. (1979) 'The remedial teacher as a change agent', in C. W. Gains and
J. M. McNicholas (eds) *Remedial Education: Guidelines for the Future.* Longman,
London.

Oliver, M. (1990) *The Politics of Disablement.* Macmillan, London.

Power, S. (1992) 'Researching the impact of education policy: difficulties and disconti-
nuities', *Journal of Education Policy,* Vol. 7, no. 5, pp. 493–500.

Quicke, J. (1986) 'A case of paradigmatic mentality? A reply to Mike Oliver', *British
Journal of Sociology of Education,* Vol. 7, pp. 81–6.

Roaf, C. and Bines, H. (eds) (1989) *Needs, Rights and Opportunities.* Falmer Press,
Lewes.

Shilling, C. (1993) 'The demise of sociology of education in Britain?', *British Journal
of Sociology of Education,* Vol. 14, no. 1, pp. 105–12.

Tejada-Flores, L. (1978) 'Games climbers play', in K. Wilson (ed.) *The Games
Climbers Play.* Diadem Books, London.

Thomas, G. (1992) 'Local authorities, special needs and the status quo', *Support for
Learning,* Vol. 7, no. 1, pp. 36–40.

Thompson, M. (1983) 'The aesthetics of risk', in J. Perrin (ed.) *Mirrors in the Cliffs*. Diadem Books, London.

Tomlinson, S. (1982) *A Sociology of Special Education*. Routledge & Kegan Paul, London.

Walford, G. (ed.) (1987) *Doing Sociology of Education*. Falmer Press, Lewes.

Walford, G. (ed.) (1991) *Doing Educational Research*. Routledge, London.

5

DISABILITY BAGGAGE: CHANGING THE EDUCATIONAL RESEARCH TERRAIN

Susan Peters

INTRODUCTION

For the past ten years, my research has focused on the social integration of students with disabilities in general education classrooms, first in the USA and later in developing countries. From the beginning I chose ethnography and participant observation as both method and process through which an understanding of social integration could be developed. Conceptually, I have taken the position that disability is a socially constructed and historically mediated process that can only be understood by stepping outside traditional approaches to research, which I feel have reproduced 'given' knowledge of disability as a medical-psychological product of innate individual traits. I believe that only a radical departure from this knowledge will affect the ways research is conducted 'on' disabled people, rather than 'for' and 'by' disabled people. In order to change the approach to study of disability, I believe people with disabilities themselves must articulate their dissatisfaction with the present conditions of education for students with disabilities, confront past failures and recognize the invalidity of the current axioms and approaches to research that prescribe unquestioning treatment of them as deviant and deficient.

Traditional methods, often reduced to strategies and techniques, ignore the importance of the social process and context of the research itself. I reason that if disability is a process of social construction, then the same characteristic may be applied to the research approach itself. From this perspective, the research method is only a tool for the conceptual framework researchers bring as baggage to the act of doing research. As a disabled person, I carry my own sets of personal and professional baggage (as every researcher carries with them into the field whether admittedly or not), but I consider this particular baggage an asset. In short, disability research, the 'disabled' researcher and the

unpacking of traditional conceptual frameworks combine to hold the possibility of a new construction of knowledge in the field of education for special
needs students.

In this chapter I therefore begin by critically examining the impact of my
personal and professional 'disability baggage' on my research framework. I
then discuss how this baggage logically led me to discard traditional baggage
of the 'other' and to develop an approach to research that uses disability as
both subject and object of research. I give examples from my own research in
the early 1980s and again in the early 1990s, showing dilemmas and insights
that developed from this research over time and across settings. I conclude
with a self-analysis of my present conceptual framework and how I feel this
analysis should guide future research, and impact the field of special education
needs.

(*Note:* In this chapter, I redefine special education needs as education of
special needs students, putting the emphasis on students, rather than needs of
'special education'. This student-centred approach is based on an ethnophilosophy of disability that is grounded in critical theory. I also reject the term
special education as tautology – all education is, or should be, special, as are all
students, for that matter.)

PLANNING THE TRIP INTO CLASSROOM
SOCIALIZATION EXPERIENCES

When I first began thinking about social integration in integrated classrooms,
I did not use the term 'socialization' at all. I began, in the summer of 1982,
by addressing policy issues of equity, cost resources, efficiency and
effectiveness. I was asking questions about equal access to programmes and
services appropriate to children's needs, the effects of cost formulas on
equality of education, the role of the federal government, the range of
services needed and kinds of retraining provided to teachers in integrated
classrooms. I was looking from the outside in, and without a theoretical
framework to guide me.

This policy perspective at the macrolevel is not surprising, considering my
then current baggage obtained from years in the political mainstream of
disability issues in the USA. My talks to various community groups focused on
'prejudiced society rife with inequities' and 'breaking down attitudinal
barriers'. I could 'see' inequities, and I could 'feel' prejudices based on attitudes
I encountered in my life as a person with a disability. The most significant of
these early experiences was my internalization of inadequacies that professionals ascribed to me during my student-teaching. (I was the only person in
the programme asked to delineate my limitations as a teacher. I was also the
only person with a disability.) My response was to prove myself by trying
harder. But I was angered by the treatment I received and also confused about

the origins of these inequities and prejudicial treatment. I was busy trying to answer the question, 'Why?'

As a doctoral student in the spring of 1983, I began investigating what I then called a 'social problems approach' to the problem of understanding societal prejudice and inequities. I was asking why 'mainstreaming' did not always result in positive social integration of students with disabilities. The questions I had asked previously had to do with the structure of society and people's attitudes. When I read a statement by Hugh Mehan (1981, p. 406) that '. . . processes operate dialectically on and through people with a cumulative effect', I began to ask, 'How?' I began to think about attitudes as an accumulation of values, preferences and unconscious assumptions that were arrived at through social experiences. I recognized that these social experiences were tied up with behaviours. Hence, the 'social problems approach' seemed to emerge as one of tying behaviours to attitudes.

Still concentrating on attitudes and how they operate to produce behaviours, I agreed with Peggy Reeves Sanday that my goal must be to '. . . describe the flow of behavior in a way that allows us to comprehend at an emotional level the events set before us and to understand the context motivating these events' (Sanday, 1982, p. 251). I felt that if I could infer a structure of feelings, attitudes and values, that these could be linked to people's choices, decisions and behaviour. My underlying assumption was that attitudes towards people with disabilities are the motivating force for behaviour.

The links between attitudes and behaviour, I reasoned, must then be a process of social interaction that I labelled as 'socialization'. I viewed socialization as an interplay of expectations and actions between individuals involved in experiencing social events. People were involved in constructing their social realities through a reflective process of assimilation and accommodation in everyday choices of practical action. A sociology of consciousness was being built through these interactions that was undoubtedly the heart of the problem of social integration. Socialization experiences were thus the give-and-take of people interacting with one another through which they built attitudes that drive their behaviour. As my own need for a sense of self-worth began to emerge, I wanted more of a positive identity. On a personal level, I began to reject the negative identity imposed on me by others and to search for ways to build a positive identity through a proactive response to prejudice. Rather than 'trying harder', I decided to 'think better'.

SELECTING THE MODE OF EXCURSION

I began the task of thinking better by building and refining socialization theory with respect to integration of students with disabilities in schools. I chose a two-pronged approach. The first item on my agenda was to re-evaluate socialization theory. The second was to select a research method that would build on my understanding of SEN practice through illumination of socialization processes in practice.

I began my field research with the assumption that attitudes were in a large measure formed by the structure of society. This belief was based on past experiences of dealing with organizations that were bureaucratically constructed effectively to shut out disabled people from opportunities to participate in work and school environments on an equal level with their peers. I approached socialization in the classroom as a function of what I called the 'structural organization of classroom learning'. I therefore suspected that the conditions needed for positive social integration in integrated classrooms could be a function of curriculum, school resources and the 'mainstreaming programme' with its policies and procedures. In a note to myself in the beginning stages of my fieldwork I wrote: 'Children with physical disabilities are just like anybody else except for certain physical differences and a receptive school environment should provide opportunities for socialization that lead to equal status and a mutual accommodation and acceptance of these differences.' I knew intuitively that people were interacting within the structures of classroom learning, but I had no idea how, and with what consequences.

As I review my field notes from my first field research experience in the USA, I am struck by the evolution of my thinking regarding socialization. My initial mode of excursion focused on the structural organization of the classroom. I had detailed diagrams of where people sat in relation to each other, lists of the activities that were scheduled for the day, minute-by-minute accounts of shifts in locations and descriptions of the physical surroundings. Part of this focus on physical environment is natural to the beginning researcher, but part of it was the baggage I still carried with me concerning the 'why' of social interaction. The teacher was a large part of my focus in the beginning. What she was doing, what she asked me to do and what kinds of activities she had the children do were a significant part of my recorded observations.

Analysis of my field notes towards the end of this first research project revealed a shift in focus from structure to communicative interaction between individual students. Much more conversation is noted, and fewer classroom conditions. Through participant observation, my focus had shifted from 'outside' structural forces to 'inside' forces of people interacting with people. Through repeated observations of classroom activities, these activities had become familiar to me and I was perhaps freer to concentrate on the 'strange' responses to these conditions manifested in the behaviour of the individuals operating within the structure of the classroom.

The method I chose to explore socialization processes described above is grounded in anthropology and the ethnography of schooling. Ethnographic methodology has been described as a naturalistic inquiry with an open-ended research design. In his discussion of ethnography in educational settings, Frank Lutz (1981, p. 52) provides a definition of ethnography as follows:

'Ethnography is a holistic, thick description of the interaction process involving the discovery of important and recurring variables in the society as they relate to one another, under specified conditions and as they affect or produce certain results and outcomes in the society.' This definition of ethnography recognizes, first, that study of a culture must be holistic, that is, more than the sum of its parts. Descriptions are placed in the context of larger purposes. The ethnographer wants to learn ways of believing, behaving and valuing members of a culture. Secondly, ethnographers eschew ethnocentric interests in order to understand other cultures on their own terms and to identify cultural patterns within the processes of both continuity and change.

The ethnographer is both the researcher and instrument of research, providing a context within a context. As a researcher, I was building theory, but I was also a participant observer in the research setting. As a result, my role as an ethnographer was inclusive in the method of analysis. In the particular school settings in which I worked, my presence and definition of myself would add substantively to the 'natural' environment. In this approach I was beginning to incorporate a new disability identity as both subject and object of research.

Specifically, my role as a participant observer in the classroom, my disability and its potential effect on the study became assets rather than liabilities. First, my ten years of experience dealing with people's reactions to my disability was a contributing factor that could be used to positive advantage. Teachers and students could profit from my experience and relate to my physical differences in a way that an 'outsider' or a 'walkie' could not. Using this capability and creating an environment of trust and non-judgemental relations through my verbal assurances and willingness to accept them on their own terms, could contribute to the teachers' understanding of their children's disabilities in the classrooms.

Secondly, my disability could affect interactions with the children under study. Children might view me as an adult role model. Children are curious and would make comparisons between me and the children with disabilities in their classroom. This curiosity and tendency to compare could be turned to advantage by stimulating discussion of the children's feelings and attitudes towards their peers.

Relations with teachers and children within the context of my disability would affect my research, but the effect would provide a basis for understanding what makes for successful social integration under certain contexts which support positive conditions for this to occur. My own struggle against negative attitudes over the past ten years made this goal imperative as a condition of research. I was determined to use my disability as the subject of research to uncover possibilities for successful integration.

Beyond the importance of myself as the instrument of research, study of individual behaviour requires a continuous process of inquiry that is focused, yet flexible. 'Because one is attempting to understand a system on its own terms, according to its own criteria of meaningfulness, one cannot predict in advance which aspects of the system will have a significance or the kind of significance they will have' (Wilcox, 1982, p. 459). As a consequence, ready-made instruments or overly precise beginning hypotheses cannot be used. Rather, part of the task of ethnographic method is to discover '. . . what is significant, what makes sense to count, and what is important to observe' (Erickson, 1977, p. 58). This approach, I felt, would be particularly powerful as a tool for breaking away from current axioms regarding disability. In essence, I was beginning to view myself (and students with disabilities) as the insiders, and non-disabled people as the 'others' or outsiders. This shift in emphasis made a significant impact on the meaning I derived from socialization theory in these early stages of my research. I began to shed the historical and outside factors of equity, efficiency and effectiveness, for a focus on 'issues of identity'.

MODIFYING THE TRIP

In my early research years I learnt a great deal about socialization processes through ethnography and participant observation in the USA. I developed an 'insiders' perspective to the problem of social integration for special needs children. I also, unconsciously, was operating at a higher level of inference. My choice of verbs at the beginning of my field experience in US classrooms described actions such as 'showing', 'asking', 'talking', 'helping'. Towards the end of my observation in these classrooms, I was focusing on individuals and describing actions such as 'tried', 'finished', 'started', 'had trouble doing', 'didn't want to'. My evolution of thinking had begun with a focus on structures and environmental conditions, and progressed towards an understanding of individual responses to these structures and conditions. I began talking about socialization as a process powered by individuals whose functional responses to their environment are socially constructed through manipulation of people, events and physical surroundings.

Throughout my initial field research I interviewed parents, students, teachers and school personnel formally and informally. I began by asking about attitudes, but quickly found that people were much more interested and articulate in talking about particular situations and their emotional responses to them. I began to see that attitudes did not consist only of people's ideals but were grounded in the choices they made when faced with the practical challenges of everyday living. I began to formulate the view that attitudes were linked to behaviours through an 'enacted curriculum', that is, attitudes and behaviours are mediated by and enacted through individual responses to environmental structures. Certain properties of these structures are given and familiar, but within these boundaries a range of choices are possible. The consequences of particular choices make the 'curriculum' or 'structure' come alive.

In the final stage of my analysis in US classrooms, I became concerned with discovering the particularities of the individual's functional responses and the conditions under which specific individuals choose certain responses over others as well as the consequences of their choices in terms of social integration. This discovery incorporated aspects of the 'outside' structure with the 'inside' responses of individuals. I discovered a rich texture of moderating processes that must somehow be linked to an analysis of the interdependent properties of the larger school environment. Socialization had come to mean a process of interaction powered by individuals within a structured environment. It was time to look beyond the classroom to a world-view of social integration in a much larger and more richly contextual environment, while still maintaining a student-centred focus.

My trip into disability research took a serendipitous turn in 1990 when I spent six weeks in Zimbabwe. I discovered that what I had conceived of as personal and professional baggage was only a veneer for the cultural baggage I carried with me. As I observed rural and urban classrooms in Zimbabwe, I became acutely aware that my study of social integration in US classrooms was ethnocentric in several major respects. First, models of schooling in the USA are essentially democratic. African schools are fundamentally meritocratic. Specifically, universal access to education is a civil right guaranteed by the US Constitution and several legislative acts. In Zimbabwe, as in many African countries, only a small percentage of students gain access to education, especially at the secondary and postsecondary levels of schooling, and access is dependent on exam performance. The consequences for students with disabilities is not trivial. Very few are able to compete successfully for available slots in the education system.

Secondly, many developing countries lack resources for education, including a lack of a suitable infrastructure to provide basic health care, transportation and physical accessibility to facilities, and other prerequisites essential for the ability to attend school. Finally, other factors such as lack of natural resources, lack of public commitment and decentralized school systems managed by non-governmental organizations (NGOs) acted as mediating variables impeding social integration.

As a result of these revelations, I began to embrace the notion of cultural boundaries or borders at a societal level. I developed the idea that beliefs about disability are transmitted through the cultural mechanism of border creations. Cultural borders are '. . . historically constructed and socially organized with maps of rules and regulations that limit and enable particular identities, individual capacities, and social forms' (Aronowitz and Giroux, 1991, p. 119). I began to see the education system as using cultural borders to establish tracks for students according to socially constructed identities based on diverse perceptions of individual ability by outsiders.

From this perspective, cultural borders manifest themselves in schools, where the educational experiences of students with disabilities are controlled to a great extent by myths and symbols which are inherent in the cultural ethos, or '. . . system of implicit and deeply internalized attitudes toward others and may be exemplified in educational practices and in activities such as parental choice of schooling based on expectations stemming from social class' (Peters, 1993, p. 23). I took note of American culture, where the prevailing notion of disability as innate deficiencies was so deeply ingrained as to remain virtually unchallenged for several decades.

I began to view socialization in the classroom not as a function of individuals' interaction and responses to others but as a terrain of struggle, power and conflict linked to central ideologies inherent in an overarching cultural framework within which schools operate.

These cultural borders manifest themselves at the individual level in a tension between ascribed and achieved attributes of individuals. I had so smugly shed the historical and social factors of equity, efficiency and effectiveness because they 'obscured' the process of socialization. Now this view seemed tantamount to heresy in the pursuit of understanding conditions needed for positive social integration. The 'inside' responses of individuals, the range of choices I thought were possible, were severely limited in the African context by forces outside the classroom. Status could not be achieved, but was ascribed by these forces. My socialization framework assumed a degree of power and control which was ignorant and, to an extent, even arrogant with respect to the larger context. This revolution in my thinking was embedded in my psyche as a result of my discussion with a disabled person in Zimbabwe. He gives an account of his educational experiences in the following excerpts from an interview (Mupindu, 1993).

On entering Grade 1:
My father was the headmaster so there was no way I could be denied an opportunity. So I did my Grade 1 and fortunately I managed to excel in terms of my academic performance. I would always take position one or two. Some people, even some children, would think it was favouritism. But when they realized that I could do the work, that's when they expected too much out of me again, because it could not be taken to be normal that I could manage.

On completion of primary school:
My father and mother didn't know what would happen to me because when I completed Grade 7, where would they take me to? After completion of Grade 7 there were scholarships that were available to the first four disabled students. And I managed to get a Beit Trust Scholarship. When I got it, the Minister would write and give you a school to go for your Form 1. But they were recommending that I go to Jairos Jiri school for vocational training. On second thought, my father thought, really, I could be tried in a secondary school environment. The Headmaster at Highfield Secondary School was white and he was very influential. He saw to it that Jairos Jiri supplied me with accommodation

and transport to and from Highfield Secondary. So I did my Form 1 and Form 2.

There I organized with two other disabled students to complain about conditions. We were termed as people who were being unthankful. Hence, my parents were summoned and they were told to take me to Jairos Jiri Center or take me home. So I went to Jairos Jiri Center.

On entering Jairos Jiri Center:
One afternoon, they were two deaf guys who were pushing me around the Center in my wheelchair. There was a school nearby where people were enrolling. It was during the liberation war and most of the schools had resorted to temporary facilities. I took my birth certificate and produced it to the headmaster and I was enrolled. Then information reached the administration that I was no longer taking leatherwork – that I was going to the secondary school. I was summoned to the office to give an explanation of why I had gone out of my way to enroll myself in secondary school. A disabled person in Jairos Jiri convinced them they should renew my scholarship, which I was entitled to. So I did my Form 3 and Form 4 there.

These first three excerpts from the interview with Ranga Mupindu exemplify the tension between ascribed and achieved attributes of people with disabilities. Teachers and students expected too little or too much. They couldn't see the 'real' Ranga. Parallels to my own experience as a student-teacher were too close for comfort. Through Ranga's eyes, I began to see the psychological and cultural genocide inherent in prejudicial and ingrained societal attitudes towards disability as innate deficiencies. Moreover, because of my own similar experiences, these attitudes were affirmed for me as crosscultural, not culture-bound phenomena.

Secondly, school is definitely a terrain of struggle, power and conflict for Ranga. Every major transition was a struggle: against stereotypes at the primary level, for access at the secondary level and against limited career goals set by professionals at the postsecondary level. At every level, Ranga fought against ascribed status. He was fortunate to have gatekeepers: his father and the headmaster at Highfield Secondary School. Without these forces fighting on his behalf, he would have, at best, remained as a leatherworker for the rest of his life. But at this point in my reconceptualization of socialization theory, I was cognizant of what I now recognized as a significant element in this struggle – Ranga's own persistence and positive self-identity. He ultimately became the Director of the National Council of Disabled Persons in Zimbabwe (NCDPZ). In this position, he is currently leading the struggle for independence and self-actualization for all people with disabilities in Zimbabwe at the societal level. His life is dedicated to addressing the issues arising from cultural borders. Ranga is between borders (socially constructed rules that limit particular identities), striving towards 'border crossings'. Specifically, border crossings beg the questions:

'Who am I?' 'Why am I here?' Border crossers challenge culture-bound rules as interlaced with questions of power, representation and identity. Ranga's experiences (ibid.) as a border crosser are revealing in the following excerpts:

On cultural barriers:
There were a lot of factors which made me really critical of our culture, because of the cultural conflicts within our culture. My grandmother thought that in order to be secure, I would need to be cleansed and the experiences were very nasty. I remember even my mother was telling me it was the only way. I was taken up to a mountain and I was left overnight on the mountain on my own. Traditional rituals were performed. It was accepted that that was the way of really helping me out. It was very terrible.

On societal attitudes:
I would say we are dealing with the type of society which doesn't consider people with disabilities as people who contribute to society. It was the same patronizing mentality [as school]. If they would do anything for people with disabilities, the politicians thought they were doing us a favor. They don't consider people with disabilities as people who have been discriminated against. They consider it to be our fate. In fact they have pity. Accordingly, even from the floor of Parliament where the issue of disability was first brought up, the MPs were quoting the Bible. Some of them started referring to cultural concepts. It showed that our political leaders are not that mature to understand the issue of disability as an important issue that should get their priorities.

On government support:
I would even say that the Act which we have is just a window-dressing type of policy measure taken by government to try and silence people with disabilities. There was nothing [in this Act] whatsoever to commit government towards empowering and removal of discrimination for persons with disabilities. It was just a way of trying to say, 'OK, we have done this in government'. But in practical terms, there is no action after policy formulation. Our Act doesn't commit government in any way to a specific course of action. Though they talk of prohibition of discrimination, they are not committed to the whole concept of disability incorporated within the bill of rights.

On allocation of educational resources:
The fact that the money is not being applied to deal with the educational requirements of people with disabilities from the early age so as to lead an independent life, really is self-defeating. Because they say you cannot be entitled to an education, you cannot be given educational opportunities. But the consequence at the end of the day of denying disabled people an education is much more expensive than provision of education. But educational opportunity is the core, really. Without an educational system you are denying and creating disabled people destitute from the outset – and illiterate destitutes, for that matter. You are creating beggars, because

if you were to interview the beggars that you find in town, I don't believe any of them have had access to education.

As a border crosser, Ranga challenges societal representations of his ascribed identity. His views of culture, government and education lay bare the need for a radical departure from current practice. The government window-dressings, patronizing mentality of schools and the denial of educational opportunity embodied in SEN that Ranga speaks of so eloquently must be eradicated. What is needed is a critical democracy that rests on the politics of identity and community.

My research focus has been on schools. Therefore, I still see the development of this critical democracy as a function of schools through the mechanism of a radical education:

> Radical education doesn't refer to a discipline or a body of knowledge. It suggests a particular kind of practice and a particular posture of questioning received institutions and received assumptions . . . The basic premises of radical education grew out of the crises in social theory . . . it has a public mission of making society more democratic.
>
> (Giroux, 1992, p. 10)

As a result of these experiences in Africa (not the least of which involved the revolution in my thinking through conversations with Ranga), I began to develop an analytical framework from which to examine the causal relations among 1) the *structure* within which disabled people experience education; 2) the common *ideologies* or values orientations prevalent in a society; and 3) schooling and related services (or lack of them) that exemplify these values in *practice*. I applied a four-step process to understand how these causal relations worked. The first step involves a description of structure, including the political economy, geographic data and demographic information such as patterns of disability as a result of climate and access to health care, organizational systems and allocation of financial and human resources. The second step entails an articulation of practice that is rooted in historical, political, economic and empirical contexts. These include an examination of national goals and priorities related to education, as well as services that support the prevailing ideology. The third step considers the ways political ideologies impact practice, including capitalist ideologies, socialist ideologies, dependency ideologies and underdeveloped socialist ideologies. (For a detailed discussion of these political ideologies, see Peters, 1993.) The fourth step applies four paradigms or models of perception of disability to structure, practice and ideology. These paradigms I view as cultural lenses of perception that underlie the consequences of educational practice. They link the tensions among political, cultural and economic spheres of influence in schools. These lenses are consistent with theories of socialization at the microlevel. But now they are also concerned at the macrolevel with the relations between people, the kinds of knowledge produced and the consequences in terms of access to education and legitimation of disabled people's social roles.

In retrospect, the social constructivist paradigm that I held so dear as the new axiom for study of disability began to fall apart under crosscultural analysis. Social constructivists have failed to effect change. Social constructivism is culture bound and based on consensus. It has been invented by 'others'. I had assumed that people with disabilities are socially oppressed. Traditionally, the key to overcoming this oppression has been based on protection of rights. But I learnt that rights are ascribed under this paradigm and thus the outcomes for people with disabilities are inherently contradictory. Specifically, political rights rest on the notion that students must be labelled in order to provide educational services. While rights are extended, they must be earned through proving disability status (i.e. deficiencies). The function of SEN and its basis in labelling is thus to impair social competence and produce dependency. I now hold the assumption that disability as a social construction must be challenged on the basis of the notion of conflict as well as the politics of self-identity.

UNPACKING DISABILITY BAGGAGE:
THE END OF THE TRIP OR THE BEGINNING?

A friend once said to me, 'Life is an adventure, not a destination'. In the context of this chapter, the following modification seems apt: 'Research is an exploration, not a finding.' The only thing that has become clear to me after ten years of research is that education for people with disabilities is a very complicated issue that goes well beyond socialization processes in the classroom. It means much more than providing a 'special' education service-delivery system. Even my chosen approach to research – ethnography and constructivist theory – has become problematic for me. From both the context and process of research – my social constructivist paradigm and my research method – two dialectic tensions have emerged.

The first tension involves ethnography itself, as the mode of research. At least, it seems the easiest of the two to define, but not necessarily the most important. The heart of ethnographic research is explication of the 'other'. Too often, the other is only the object of discourse in social science. Ethnography and its source, the discipline of anthropology, have given us the legacy of the Native Savage. Parallels to the lame, crippled, deviant other are too close for comfort. Bringing the personal experience of disability to the research process has its advantages. However, it has been noted that '. . . the anthropologist "invents" the culture he [or she] believes himself [or herself] to be studying, that the relation is more "real" for being his [or her] particular acts and experiences than the thing it relates' (Mudimbe, 1988, p. 27).

In other words, the danger in ethnography, lies in seeing what one wants to see and in the limitations of an 'open mind'. A good ethnographer takes great care to triangulate data and to search for contradictions to observed events. My experience has led me to the conclusion that these techniques need to combine with an intense level of personal introspection regarding the baggage I spoke of earlier. This introspection necessitates a dialectic tension between creative discourses and the epistemological field which makes them possible. Otherwise, the method becomes the force driving the discourse. This tension works both ways, however. There is an equal danger that the conceptual framework will reign supreme over a scientific solution to the research problem. A solution may lie in the direction of viewing people with disabilities not as functional objects but as the starting-point of discourse.

This last statement leads me to the second dialectical tension I discovered for myself in the course of my research. In defining this tension more precisely, I turn to the work of V. Y. Mudimbe in *The Invention of Africa* (1988). In his insightful discussion of gnosis, philosophy and the order of knowledge, Mudimbe asserts that '. . . racial identity stands as an absolute precondition for any sociopolitical transformation of Africa' (ibid., p. 131). He argues that so much symbolic violence has been done to Africans in the name of scientific research (and particularly through ethnography) that a new order of knowledge can only emerge from Africans who challenge their ascribed identities in bold new ways.

I propose that the same argument can be made for understanding disability. Our struggle as an oppressed minority must entail a re-examination of the discourse – even social constructivism. First, because this paradigm has failed to effect change. Secondly, it is culture bound and based on consensus. Finally, the discourse has been invented to a large extent by others. Those of us with disabilities who know what it means to be disabled in the most basic sense of the word must put forward a disability consciousness which drives creative discourse.

A disability consciousness must evolve through an analytical synthesis of cultural borders on the one side, and contradictions created by existing paradigms on the other. This synthesis means no less than a struggle for liberation. An ethnophilosophy of disability needs to emerge in the field of disability research characterized by two features: 1) a break with the ideology of the other inherent in ethnographic techniques; and 2) a renewed questioning of: 'Who is a person with a disability? How does one describe him or her? For what purpose?'

An insider's perspective is necessary to accomplish this ethnophilosophy. In the words of Ranga Mupindu, Zimbabwean disabled activist:

> Because of our militancy, we have been criticized for contributing to our suffering and our discrimination. But I would say that characteristic of ourselves is a very positive one if ever we are to change the situation, because there is no revolution that has been fought passively and has been won. I mean, even the able-bodied rely on military strategies to do a lot of

things in order for them to win in their objectives or to achieve their political requirements. And disabled persons have been expected to beg for
rights. We should not accept it. We are saying to ourselves, 'We have got
to take a lead in addressing and redressing the situation'. And we need to
conscientize everybody to understand that it's a struggle for ALL. But
being spearheaded by the people affected. We are the people who know
what it means to be disabled. The others can't imagine. They can only
dream. They don't even see what sort of discrimination we are experiencing because they are not disabled.

These words constitute the consciousness and the voice of disabled people
which is a beginning basis for an ethnophilosophy that must become the
driving force behind the discourse in the field of disability research.

In suggesting a course of action for future research in SEN, I again draw
from Mudimbe and his proposal for overcoming the psychological oppression
of black Africans. Five components for a new discourse in disability research
are necessary:

1. The existence of a group of philosophers with disabilities living and
   working in an intellectually stimulating cultural milieu resolutely open to
   new possibilities in the lives of disabled people.
2. A substantive and critical use of external philosophical 'reflectors', which,
   through the patience of discipline, would promote disability in a universal
   and crosscultural framework of thought.
3. A selective and flexible inventory of values as they relate to disability –
   including attitudes, categories and symbols – which would possibly
   provoke thought in the sense of building a new sociopolitical philosophy of
   disability based on a critical examination of both the past and the future of
   people with disabilities.
4. A clear dissociation of the researchers' scientific baggage from cultural
   baggage which would amplify major contrasts (e.g. I versus the Other,
   nature versus nurture, deviance versus oppression).
5. An examination of SEN researchers' main temptations – choices of educational systems apparently in accordance with disabled people's urgent needs
   (as in the case of special education, which has become an end in itself).

The above components for a new discourse or ethnophilosophy of disability
might begin by addressing some basic questions and assumptions. First,
virtually everyone experiences physical or mental limitations either early or
later in life. Instead of focusing our energies on preventing the inevitable, how
can we weave our disabilities (if they are disabilities) into the fabric of all our
lives, rather than reducing them to isolated traits or innate deficiencies? The
above question must be answered 'Because the pursuit of "other" is
inextricably linked with sense of self . . . a limited understanding of self
continues to restrict scope and possibility within the comparative education
field' (Epstein, 1994, p. 10). Further, '. . . an unwillingness to consider the way

in which the body is treated on an everyday basis limits our ability to examine issues of identity, personhood, their social construction, and their potential transformation' (ibid., p. 24). Certainly, my own and Ranga's struggle for positive self-identity, in conflict with socially constructed identities, make this question imperative for potential transformation of the field of SEN.

Secondly, the recent integration model of SEN is at base an unconscious rejection of disabled people's positive self-identity. The 'positive role models' that SEN seeks to expose people with disabilities to in general education classrooms (in order to emulate the 'other') are not always or often the paragons of behaviour that we assume them to be. Therefore, the purpose behind integration for disabled people as presently conceived is a symbolically violent act. It excludes the possibility that disabled people may be positive role models from which others may emulate their behaviour. (In this regard, I am further indebted to Irving Epstein's insightful treatise, 'Comparative education: the search for other through the escape from self', 1994.)

Relative to the above assumption, some people with ascribed disabilities choose to embrace their difference as a positive identity marker. They derive power from their differences and assume the role of border crossers. This identity is often developed in the absence of familial role models and in the presence of culture-bound ascribed deficiencies. For these powerful individuals, the social structure influences without strictly determining beliefs and behaviours. How does this transformation occur? Under what circumstances? The politics of identity and community that I described earlier need closer scrutiny in this regard.

The impact of the call for new ethnophilosophy of disability on the field of SEN is potentially significant. It challenges virtually all of the assumptions and premises on which SEN has been built over the past several decades. The capability for change ultimately rests with the authentic voices of people with disabilities. As Joshua Malinga (Secretary General of Disabled Persons International) said during his speech to Zimbabwean SEN professionals in response to the question, 'Why haven't attitudes changed in 2000 years?': 'Nothing changes until those who feel the pain decide, "Enough is enough!"' Ranga and I and many others like us have decided enough is enough. Our collective voices must lead the way in addressing and redressing issues of personhood, self-identity and self-worth. Resolving these issues at the microlevel are preconditions for addressing the macrolevel issues of equity, access and discrimination that currently dominate the SEN research agenda. The field of SEN will succeed in addressing these issues to the extent that it opens its doors to the ideas, leadership and critical analyses of the traditionally marginalized people it has sought to serve: those with disabilities. This leadership is essential for our liberation from current SEN practices – practices that have failed to recognize the most basic element of our struggle: our personhood.

I began this chapter with an examination of the impact of my disability baggage on my research in the field of disability. My journey through time and across settings has taken several turns, ending where I began – with the need to address issues of equity, access and discrimination. I can still see inequities and feel prejudices. However, the knowledge I have gained along the way has equipped me for my next trip – into the realm of new discoveries and new discourses. In preparation for the next trip, I will pack my 'liberation' baggage.

REFERENCES

Aronowitz, S. and Giroux, H. A. (1991) *Postmodern Education: Politics, Culture and Social Criticism*. University of Minnesota Press: Minneapolis, Minn.

Epstein, I. (1994) 'Comparative education: the search for other through the escape from self.' Paper presented at the 1994 Annual Meeting of the Comparative and International Education Society, San Diego, Calif. (quoted with permission).

Erickson, F. (1977) 'Some approaches to inquiry in school-community ethnography', *CAE Newsletter*, Vol. 8, no. 2, pp. 58–69.

Giroux, H. (1992) *Border Crossings: Cultural Workers and the Politics of Education*. Routledge, Chapman & Hall, New York.

Lutz, F. (1981) 'Ethnography – the holistic approach to understanding schooling', in Green and Wallat (eds) *Ethnography and Language in Educational Settings*. Ablex Publishing, Norwood, NJ.

Mehan, H. (1981) 'Identifying handicapped students', in S. B. Bacharach (ed.) *Organizational Behavior in Schools and School Districts*. Praeger, New York.

Mudimbe, V. Y. (1988) *The Invention of Africa: Gnosis, Philosophy, and the Order of Knowledge*. Indiana University Press: Bloomington, Ind.

Mupindu, R. (1993) Transcript of taped interview with Susan Peters. Harare, Zimbabwe, 1 June.

Peters, S. (1987) 'Mainstreaming and socialization of exceptional children.' UMI Dissertation Information Service, Ann Arbor, Mich.

Peters, S. (1993) 'An ideological-cultural framework for the study of disability', in S. Peters (ed.) *Education and Disability in Cross-Cultural Perspective*. Garland Publishing, New York.

Sanday, P. R. (1982) 'Anthropologists in schools: school ethnography and ethnography', in P. Gilmore and A. Glatthorn (eds) *Children in and out of School*. Center for Applied Linguistics, Washington, DC.

Wilcox, K. (1982) 'Ethnography as a methodology', in G. Spindler and L. Spindler (eds) *Doing the Ethnography of Schooling*. Holt, Rinehart & Winston, New York.

6

CONSTRUCTING PARTICIPATORY RESEARCH: IN PRINCIPLE AND IN PRACTICE

John Swain

THE FOUNDATIONS

The Context

This chapter is a critical reflection on a study of student participation in the decision-making processes which shape their education and their lives. I undertook the research in Elmtree College, which was a newly established, supposedly unique, segregated college, offering 'vocational education' for 14–18-year-olds with 'special education needs'. Data was collected covering a five-and-a-half-year period from the first official proposal for the college to the end of the second year of operation. The college incorporated many recent 'new vocational' educational initiatives and espoused many features which aspired to democratic ideals in management, ethos and aims (Swain, 1993).

The college was opened as part of a reorganization of special educational needs provision in the city, which largely involved a move away from all-age special schools through closing some segregated institutions and opening others. I initially approached the then Adviser for Special Education, who was later to become the Principal of Elmtree College, with a vague idea of conducting research and was welcomed with enthusiasm. For me, however, the feeling was one of considerable trepidation fuelled by a lack of clarity about the whole enterprise of 'research', which was relatively new to me, and what I saw as the fundamental problematic nature of the project.

The starting-point for my thinking was a belief about the nature of 'special educational needs'. It was not a term I could then, or now, easily define. My belief was, however, that 'special educational needs' are produced in decision-making processes which marginalize, disempower and 'dis-able' a section of the school population. This had been repeatedly confirmed through experience of the hierarchical nature of special schools. From this the direction of the research emerged slowly, painfully slowly, and I was to find myself still rewriting the specific aims even at the stage of the final write-up. The first glimmers came from these existing beliefs and the overall focus centred on participation in decision-making. But as this clarified I increasingly questioned my role as a researcher and encountered a dilemma which would endure throughout the research. It seemed to me that I was entering through a different door and engaging in the very social relations in which special educational needs are constructed. Even at the initial point of access, entry had been gained through the Principal and imposed on all the other participants. Participation was to become not only the substantive focus of the study I wanted to undertake but also my focus for conceiving and evaluating the process of research itself. Eventually it dawned on me, as I shall attempt to convey in this chapter, that the latter was a reflection of the former.

At the outset I knew there was an acknowledged lack of knowledge of the meaning of 'special educational needs' from the viewpoint of those involved: their experiences; their intentions and desires; and their understandings. The case and the urgent need for research into participants' viewpoints has been argued a number of times in the literature (Corrie and Zakluiewicz, 1985; Barton, 1988). The 'participatory research' I set out to construct with the participants at Elmtree College went further than this, however. It was to be research in which the meaning of 'special educational needs' was not only constructed through the experiences and understanding of participants but the participants would also have a say in the planning and control of the process of construction.

This study of student participation involved a programme which was itself designed to promote participation in the process of research and to provide a forum for negotiating meanings, ideological critique and empowerment of participants at Elmtree College. It was this struggle for such participatory research and the whole problematic process of turning principles into practice which came (and continues) to dominate my thinking, dilemmas and personal satisfactions and despairs as a researcher. This chapter, then, is about the principles and practice, and possibilities and limitations of doing research *with* rather than *on* people (Reason and Heron, 1986).

Good intentions

More recent literature has documented a number of relevant approaches that claim to be essentially 'participatory', including: 'research-as-praxis' (Lather, 1986), 'democratic research' (Hall, 1981), 'critical research' (Comstock, 1982) and 'emancipatory action research' (Carr and Kemmis, 1986). Furthermore, the term 'participatory research' is itself being increasingly used to denote a particular research methodology (French 1993) and the term 'co-researcher' used to refer to people who are the subjects of research (Atkinson and Shakespeare, 1993). However, in conceiving and planning this particular study I increasingly found that good intentions opened up a catalogue of challenging questions.

The most radical justification for participatory research challenges structures and power relations both within and through processes of research. In these terms participatory research is directed towards supporting the struggle of oppressed groups and political activities to secure equal opportunities and improved quality of life. This has been articulated from the viewpoint of disabled people by Oliver (1992, pp. 110–11):

> The emancipatory paradigm, as the name implies, is about the facilitating of a politics of the possible by confronting social oppression at whatever levels it occurs . . . This does then mean that the social relations of research production do have to be fundamentally changed; researchers have to learn how to put their knowledge and skills at the disposal of their research subjects, for them to use in whatever way they choose.

This line of justification is applicable to the present research given the role of segregated education in the marginalization of groups of young people. However, there are some complex issues. Though there were many examples of 'student resistance' (Giroux, 1983) within the college, the idea that the students could be described as people who had 'decided to empower themselves' was extremely questionable. Furthermore, in all but exceptional cases the students at the college were non-disabled young people from working-class families and many were from backgrounds of extreme poverty and deprivation. Though these young people faced considerable oppression of different forms, few would have been identified, by themselves or others, as disabled people and few would identify themselves as having 'special educational needs'.

Zarb (1992, p. 128) argues that 'Simply increasing participation and involvement will never by itself constitute emancipatory research unless and until it is disabled people themselves who are controlling the research and deciding who should be involved and how'. Such claims could not be made for the participation and involvement of the students in the present research (and hence the use of the term 'participatory' rather than 'emancipatory' in this chapter). The participation was at my initiation and discretion, and under my ultimate control. Participation was my intention, not necessarily the participants', students' or teachers'.

Over the two to three years in the field at Elmtree College many strategies were adopted to develop participatory research. In principle 'participation' underpinned decision in the construction of many aspects of this research, including access, sampling, methods of data collection and analysis, and field relations. This included the use of repeated open-ended interviews which used counselling techniques to facilitate participants in exploring and developing their feelings and understanding about themselves and their social world. These interviews were largely conducted by myself as 'the researcher', but as a further strategy to promote participation both teachers and students were involved as interviewers. Analysis was conceived and undertaken as integral to the whole process of research and to the dialogue between myself and the participants. This was a cumulative process developed over a number of stages, particularly through the use of 'reflection documents' which were used both as a means of feedback to participants and as a catalyst for further dialogue.

There are, however, no clear strategies for linking the tenets of theory and the practice of research. This is a problematic area for any research in the social sciences. Guidelines for developing a participatory research design are rare and raise many problematic questions. For instance, Tripp (1983, p. 44) states that his paper on 'coauthorship and negotiation' in interviews is '. . . rather a description of a point of departure than of a destination'. In her review of relevant literature, Lather (1986, p. 265) also admits that '. . . there are at present few research designs which encourage negotiating meaning beyond the descriptive level'. In the context of the present study, it should be added that examples of full democratic research designs which include full reciprocal participation by young people are unavailable in the literature. In general terms, the search for a participatory research design is, to use Lather's (1986) words, 'a journey into uncharted territory', and the above list of strategies represents only 'points of departure'.

In the remainder of the chapter this critical reflection on the conversion of principles to practice will be developed through a number of stages:

1. An analysis of the nature of the research as it was experienced and understood by participants.
2. An analysis of the field relations established within the research.
3. A consideration of the criteria which need to be brought to bear in analysing the validity of participatory research.
4. Some closing thoughts on participation from my viewpoint.

WHOSE CONSTRUCTION?

Throughout the study of student participation the process of the research itself was a focus for discussion between myself, as the researcher, and the staff and students at Elmtree. Indeed, the research itself was seen as being constructed in this dialogue. The following is an analysis of participants' responses to and reflections on the research as a whole, that is, the 'meaning of research' as it was experienced and understood by participants in this study.

The data on which the following analysis is based has been drawn from all the field notes, interview transcripts and the research diary throughout every stage of the research. A search was undertaken for references to the research by participants, a list of relevant quotes compiled and a content analysis was carried out.

As part of the establishment of a new institution

The initial response from participants was, I felt, a general welcoming of both myself and the idea that research was being undertaken. This was stated in the most explicit terms by George Goode, the Principal at the college: 'I'm glad you're here.' The fact that research was being carried out was seen as adding to the status of the college: '[The research], of course, is important for me because they see this as an important little college, important enough for someone to do research here.' The research was mentioned in official documentation (including the college audit), and was included as an item for the agenda for the second meeting of the Staff Council. I was officially introduced at the first full staff meeting (before the college had opened), and was provided with a room, with my name on the door and a desk. The welcome from the other members of staff was equally evident as indicated, for instance, by the invitations to the researcher to participate in meetings of groups of staff, such as to plan areas of the curriculum.

One crucial feature of the whole context here was that this was a newly established institution. Thus all the participants in the college were establishing new relationships and the researcher was not seen as an 'outsider'. It was also a period of some apprehension in which the research could be seen as potentially useful for participants. Brian Woods (Deputy Principal) states: 'I would appreciate that feedback because we're going into something new and there are going to be pitfalls.' The newness of the college, however, could also be a feature of participants' concerns about the research. The first interview with Colin Trent (T – teacher), for instance, was punctuated with such phrases as 'we don't know yet, do we?'

As evaluation

A dominant view of the research by teachers was as an evaluation of the college and themselves, despite my repeated statements to the contrary. Though rarely voiced, such a perspective could also be found in statements by students, as illustrated in the following exchange with Ian Hargreaves:

Ian (S – student): Excuse me, sir, what exactly is your role in the college?
John (R – researcher): I'm here looking at how the college works. I'm trying to get people's views about the college. I'd be very interested in what you think.

Ian (S): I presume you're interested in those statements, what I'm like, what I'm not like, ticking boxes. Trying to find out what makes me tick, like.

Participants also felt my presence changed the situation and thus the experiences and behaviours of those present during 'participant observation'. Jane White (T), for instance, states: 'I'm not like that usually. I can joke on with them and they are different too, asking questions and that.' Such apprehensions could be seen as couching the research within hierarchical power relations within the college, recognizing the micropolitical nature of research. This emerged too in participants' views of the research as providing 'answers' or 'recommendations'. Nigel Moore (T) asked about my recommendations from the research, but then went on to say that he did not think any recommendations would be listened to or acted on by the top levels of the management team.

Inherent within participants' views relating to the research as evaluation was not only conceptions of the nature of research but also conceptions of the power structures and decision-making processes within the college. Within the hierarchical structure, the research was seen as holding two contradictory possibilities: as an appraisal of their work as teachers and thus potentially threatening; and as a means of conveying their views to affect decision-making in the college, and thus potentially liberating.

As an impartial account

Having said that I was in many ways not treated as an 'outsider', many responses to the research, and particularly the reflection documents, had connotations of 'impartiality'. George Goode (the Principal) states: 'It's been very, very useful. I mean quite apart from answering your own questions you've served a very important touchstone for the staff to have a neutral observer, particularly a non-judgemental one who's prepared to listen and write down what they say.' As illustrated in the following quote from Mike Ball (T), there was a belief in the need for a 'neutral voice' in collating the views of participants:

> I thought it was very worth while. I mean it's nice to have the views not just of the students and the staff but the views of someone looking from outside as well. I know that you're putting forward our views but they're having to respond to the questions you are putting to them. I know some staff have been very interested in reading all of this.

This view of the research and of my role was a particularly strong feature of teachers' responses to the first reflection document. The first stage of the research had been one of establishing field relations and access, and this document referred to some apprehensions. The style and approach to analysis in this feedback to staff enabled the document itself to play a role in easing anxieties associated with perceptions of research as a form of evaluation, and to play a related role in strengthening field relations. The following quotes are illustrative:

> I think it's important that all the views are aired and no one's been identified as saying this, that or the other.
>
> (Mike Ball, T)

> Oh, it's very interesting and very supportive I thought. I mean, I enjoyed the fact that it was value free, even though knowing you fairly well I would have thought that there are lots of things here that you have views about but you kept them out.
>
> (George Goode, Principal)

As a realistic reflection

Closely related to the views of impartiality was the perception of reflection documents as a true or valid analysis of participants' views and experiences at Elmtree College. The veracity of the reflection documents was only questioned on one occasion. Mike Ball (T) raised a number of points on the basis that the situation had changed since the interviews on which the documents were based had been conducted. Otherwise none of the participants suggested either that their views and experiences were not reflected, or that the analyses were based on misunderstandings or distorted interpretations. Indeed, the reflection documents were repeatedly accepted as 'true reflections', as illustrated by the following quotes:

> Your observations are very realistic and truthful.
>
> (Brian Woods, T)

> I thought it was a pretty comprehensive sort of survey really. Over the short space of time that you've been here you seem to have got the general idea of what's going on from everybody, either your observations or what people have actually told you. I thought this one here, the general areas of concern, I thought they were quite er . . . realistic.
>
> (Patricia Newton, T)

> I found it very interesting. I mean lots of things you were saying, dimensions of approaches, of freedom, choice, compulsion, are things that I'm aware of being there and now you've separated them out.
>
> (George Goode, Principal)

As an aid to further reflection

Closely related to perception of the 'neutrality' and the 'veracity' of the research were views of the research as promoting reflection and dialogue. In relation to the reflection documents, such views again couched the research within the immediate context of Elmtree College and, in particular, the pressures on teachers and the lack of forums for discussion. Catherine Even (T) states, for instance:

> Actually as you flick through it . . . I don't know . . . perhaps things are not as negative as we think. Especially as I've been feeling the last few days. And it was nice to think that perhaps there's other people feeling the same as you did. We see so little of one another as a staff we don't know how other people are feeling.

For some participants, the framework of analysis was useful in this respect:

> The way you've done it, on the one hand, on the other hand, on the third hand, yes that's a useful way of doing it. Looking at the three there they seem to make sense. At sometime or other I come to see each month the dilemmas you're talking about, particularly in the sense of problems.
>
> (George Goode, Principal)

> It's interesting now we can look at this and we can say there is a pattern there . . . there are things we haven't thought about.
>
> (Mike Ball, T)

> And I think it's a way of getting across a message as well, without anyone actually saying I think you should be doing this or that. The messages come through loud and clear without any aggravation or upset. I think that's useful too.
>
> (Catherine Even, T)

As a counselling process

Participants made many references to the process of research in ways which point to parallels with counselling processes. Elements of this type of conception of the research have already emerged in the views discussed above. That is to say, the research has emerged as a process which, to an extent at least, is non-judgemental; accurately reflects the views of participants; and yet is challenging in enabling participants to develop and re-evaluate their views. Some participants pointed to more detailed aspects of this conception of the research. First, there was the opportunity to talk to a 'sympathetic ear' outside institutional roles and relationships, as pointed to by Brian Woods (Deputy Principal): 'I appreciate the chance to talk to someone when you're not seen as the Vice Principal and having an axe to grind. You've raised a lot of points.' Sometimes the process of the research was seen by participants as 'counselling' in the sense of enabling participants to overcome problems such as those associated with stress: 'I mean in that sense of just venting things, a trouble shared is a trouble halved. But equally self-esteem things . . .' (George Goode, Principal). Catherine Even (T) talked about the process of being interviewed as a cathartic experience: 'It's a good job you were here this morning, the way I was feeling. It really helps to get it off your chest.' It could also be, more simply, a generally enjoyable experience, as is evident in a number of the above quotes. I would sometimes be sought out by staff wishing to discuss an issue they considered to be of importance. Students would also sometimes want to know when I was, 'gan interview me again?'

As the involvement of the researcher in the daily life of Elmtree College

For some participants, mainly students, though also some non-teaching staff, the research had no meaning beyond my presence and involvement at Elmtree College. This was a dimension of the research for all participants as, for instance, in informal situations (such as in the dining-room), working with me as a co-teacher or as the teacher of video-making courses. This was reflected in my own dilemmas in making use of some of the data, particularly data collected in contexts in which I was obviously being related to as a friend, confidant or a colleague, rather than as a 'researcher'.

A critical reflection

At one level, this analysis of the participants' conceptions of the research provides a picture of the nature of the research. While I set out with the intention that the research should be participatory, the participants differed greatly in their views of the whole nature of the research. Some conceptions did seem to be consistent with my intentions, but some, particularly as 'evaluation', were the antithesis. At another level, however, this analysis reflects vital questions I confronted relating to conducting supposedly participatory research in the specific context of special educational needs. Overall it became increasingly apparent that conceptions of research were constructed within the existing power relations and ideologies within the college, whatever 'good intentions' I had. I can pinpoint three main themes in my struggles to establish participation in research:

1. The research was not conceived by the participants as a forum for questioning the nature of 'special education needs' or even the very existence of Elmtree College as a segregated provision. Whatever the form of 'participation' recognized in the participants' understanding of the

research process, the dominant ideology of special education needs in many ways stood in opposition to critical discussions about the social and historical context of the college.

2. There was little in this analysis of the views of students. Throughout the research, though, there was a great deal of data from which I could reflect on the views of students, there was little to suggest that they felt themselves to be conscious participants in controlling the research process. For students, participation seemed to mean involvement with me personally even when this involved specific activities such as planning and conducting interviews with each other about their experiences at Elmtree. This became a real dilemma for me as a researcher: 'participation', which I saw as crucial to the nature of the research I was pursuing, could mean compliance and acceptance by students. The conduct of the research furthered the very social relations of special educational needs that I wished to question.

3. Finally, extending the above points, the participants' conceptions of the research, and also my own, built on existing concepts of relationships within the college. Conceptions of the research as 'counselling', significantly, furthered the ideology that the effectiveness, justification and *raison d'être* of the college lay in the quality of relationships between staff and students. It is to the conceptions of relationships which I shall now turn, particularly my understanding of 'field relations'.

BUILDING RELATIONS

Consideration of 'field relations', and in particular the development of democratic and reciprocal relationships between the researcher and researched/co-researchers, lies at the heart of participatory research. The main framework for understanding and realizing field relations in qualitative research generally has been that of 'researcher roles', and particularly a participatory–non-participatory dimension in possible stances available to researchers in qualitative research. One much-quoted model identifies four possible roles: 'complete participant'; 'participant as observer'; 'observer as participant'; and 'complete observer'. The 'complete participant', for instance, becomes a member of the group and hides his or her identity as a researcher.

It can be argued that there are three major limitations to such analyses of researcher involvement. First, as argued by Woods (1986), all researchers 'participate' in their research whatever methods are employed. Conceptions of 'non-participation' can distract from reflections on power in field relations, in that they invoke connotations of 'neutrality'. Secondly, such notions of role define relationships by default, focusing exclusively on the involvement of the researcher. The 'researched', as this particular term implies, are simply assumed to be the objects of research with no active participation in constructing the research process. Thirdly, conceptions of researcher involvement in terms of roles might also restrict his or her participation in the research process. Writing about different forms of interviews, Woods (1986, p. 67) states his preference for conversations and discussions '. . . wherein people can be "themselves" and not feel bound by roles'. Though he seems to be referring exclusively to people who are the subjects of research, his statement could apply equally to researchers.

A different basis is required, therefore, for reflecting on the quality of field relations in participatory research. In this study I turned to humanistic psychology for an alternative. The framework of three qualities of relationships (genuineness, acceptance and empathy) was first described by Rogers in the 1940s and has since been developed in many of his works (for instance, Rogers, 1978). It is briefly summarized below together with some relevant strategies adopted and barriers faced in this research.

Genuineness/realness

Genuineness involves the possibility of 'being yourself' in a relationship and in communication. It is a sharing of true feelings and attitudes, or mutual self-disclosure. In this sense it implies flexibility of expectations so that neither person is 'playing a role'. When the expectations of both participants are rigidly defined communication is not 'genuine'.

Shakespeare (1993, p. 98) has discussed her attempts to be 'genuine' in the sense of '. . . underplaying my role as a researcher and emphasizing my role as an ordinary person'. This involved self-disclosure in conversations. I found that I too strived for such personal genuineness, and went some way to achieving it in many relationships (for example, with the member of staff who travelled with me each morning to the college). It was more difficult to achieve with participants who had more rigid views and expectations of me as 'the researcher'.

A second approach to establishing genuineness in field relations was through openness with regard to the aims and processes of the research. The general intention was to establish 'open' research in which participants had a say over when and how they became involved and had open access to all information and analyses generated by the research. One strategy to establish openness was the use of explanatory documents which 1) provided some explanation of the research; 2) invited people to participate; and 3) invited questions about the research.

Though I was uncomfortable about it, I thought it was inappropriate and, it has to be admitted, impractical, to disseminate these documents to students, and verbal explanations and discussions were mainly relied on to secure openness in relationships with students. Nevertheless, documents were used in the group interview sessions with students, which similarly emphasized confidentiality. Furthermore, it was hoped that the use of students as interviewers would facilitate openness, in that students may be more genuine with their fellow students than with staff or myself.

One strategy for encouraging openness was confidentiality, on the grounds that secrecy of identity would enable participants to be open with me without possible anxieties about disclosures being made public. The establishment of openness and confidentiality in research encompassed a number of unforeseen problems, in that commitments to concealing the identity of participants and of the college itself could not be completely and unquestioningly met. Whatever pseudonyms were used it would not be possible to prevent a determined and interested person from following up all the clues to discover both the true identity of the college and hence the identity of staff and students. For those inside the college, tracing the identity of participants would be that much easier.

Acceptance/respect/unconditional positive regard

This is acceptance and trust in a relationship. It involves communicating that the other person is a worthwhile, unique and capable person. Acceptance in communication involves accepting that the other person has a point of view which, whether you agree with it or not, is valid to that person and worth listening to. It also involves communicating the degree of commitment to the relationship and its importance to the people concerned.

The whole process of research was conceived of, pursued and analysed as a process of active listening. This was not simply an intensive involvement with participants in face-to-face situations but was also realized through transcribing interviews, reading and rereading the transcripts, and reflecting back the results of analyses to further the research dialogue. One important aspect in the present research, which has received little mention in the literature, was long personal conversations, between myself and both students and staff, which had no apparent direct relevance to the study of student participation. For instance, one member of staff talked to me in length about problems with her back, another about running his private business and a third about moving house. One student talked about his collection of computer games, another about his favourite film stars and others talked about *Neighbours*, the television programme. Such conversations can appear time consuming and irrelevant, but they seemed to me to play an important part in establishing acceptance.

One complicating factor in acceptance was the existing roles within the college in relationships between staff, between students and particularly between staff and students. I felt this was especially difficult in my relationships with some of the students. Burgess's (1984) assertion that any adult appearing in school must, in students' eyes, have some strong connection with the teaching profession was substantiated in this research. One obvious manifestation of this was in regard to my responses in controlling students. For instance, during one of the earlier video-making sessions in which I was co-teaching, one student repeatedly expressed his desire and intention to take the video camera into one of the local shops to 'film the Pakis', leading eventually to conflict between myself and the student over his repeated use of racist language. Nevertheless, I also found that it was easier to form relationships with students when I was perceived as a teacher rather than having, from their viewpoint, an indiscriminate undefined role.

Empathy

Empathy is a shared understanding and sensitivity between two people. 'Putting yourself in the shoes of another' and 'seeing through the eyes of another' are ways of describing empathy. It involves both feeling and understanding situations and events from the viewpoint of participants.

I saw 'immersion' as integral to the process of building empathy with the participants at Elmtree College. In relationships with staff this included co-teaching at the college. It was considerably more difficult for me to 'see through the eyes' of students. This was in part achieved by listening to students' viewpoints; being in sessions without a recognized teaching role; and involvement in informal activities, such as lunch-times, when teacher and student roles carried more flexible expectations.

One set of issues in establishing empathy lay within my perception of myself as a 'researcher' and of the process of research. Such issues are usually discussed in the literature under conceptions of 'going native' and 'marginality'. At heart this is a dilemma between going native, that is, identifying with participants' viewpoints to the extent that the task of analysis is abandoned in favour of the joys or anxieties of actual participation; and being marginal, that is, maintaining a social and intellectual distance between myself and the participants at Elmtree. One specific instance of this was in defining the nature of 'participatory research'. Going native meant pursuing the participants' view of research as evaluation. This would have involved monitoring the effectiveness of the college in realizing the stated aims. On the other hand, being marginal meant engaging both students and staff in questioning the nature, purposes and even the existence of this segregated institution. Thus I felt a dissonance between pursuing my conception of research as a critical dialogue and empathizing with the views of many of the participants about the nature of the research.

A critical reflection

At one level, this analysis of 'building relations' again reflects the degree to which my 'good intentions' were realized. While I set out to establish non-hierarchical social relations in this research, analysis of the quality of actual relationships suggested a much more complex picture. At another level, however, critical questions arise which speak to the specific context of special educational needs. Overall, it became clear within the research that the context itself (expectations, existing relationships, structures and so on) was not only the focus for the research but also shaped and defined the research processes themselves. In terms of my endeavours to establish participation three critical points emerge:

1. This conception remains at the level of personal and, basically, one-to-one relationships. It is individualized as in nearly all definitions of 'special educational needs'. Any notion of empowerment in the above analysis can only be conceived in individual terms, rather than notion of group solidarity or emancipation. As in Elmtree College generally, in the research it was personal relationships with individuals which was given paramount importance.
2. As a researcher I found myself relating to people as individuals (except in the context of timetabled sessions for students) rather than groups with vested interest. As in the ideology of special educational needs, no recognition can be given to inequalities between groups of people or to conflicts of interest between sections of society. In particular, in Elmtree there was no forum for debate, either formal or informal, for either the staff or the students and this was reflected in the research.
3. Finally, I saw participation as founded on personal relationships between myself and the participants. This reflects the importance given to personal relationships between students and teachers in the context of special educational needs generally. The problem I faced, particularly in relation to students, was that there is no such thing as a neutral position for a researcher in a hierarchical institution. Furthermore, the data from different sources collected at Elmtree consistently suggested a strong association between the quality of teacher–student relationships and mechanisms of the social control of students.

BUILDING EVALUATION

In some respects the circumstances of this research into student participation in decision-making were favourable to the pursuit of a participatory approach. It was significant, for instance, that this was a PhD study, there was no funding-body and I had full control over the form and direction of the research, ostensibly at least. I was thus in a position to attempt to share the control with the participants. Nevertheless, as evident in the analysis above, the realization of participation in practice is fraught with complex issues. 'Participatory' is another one of those terms, replete in the special educational needs literature, which can be more to do with strengthening dominant ideologies and the illusion of change than real shifts of power. Research can be liberating and it can be oppressive, and there were elements of both in this particular study. Critical evaluation, which should also be conducted as a participatory process, is essential, particularly in relation to the validity of the research processes themselves (i.e. in what sense that might be said to be 'participatory').

In relation to 'research-as-praxis', Lather (1986) calls for a redefining of the concept of validity, along the lines of what she calls 'catalytic validity', that is, '. . . the degree to which the research process reorients, focuses, and energies participants toward knowing reality in order to transform it' (p. 272). In a similar way, participatory research requires a re-examination of the concept of 'validity' to complement the redefinition of research processes such as 'field relations'. In this light, a possible framework of three questions for a critique of participatory research was developed through the research itself. To draw this critical reflection together, then, the following is an analysis of this study of student participation in a special educational needs context as participatory research using these criteria.

Does the research promote both self-realization and mutual understanding through dialogue? As reflected in the above analysis of the participants' and my own perceptions of the research process, there was evidence that the research at Elmtree did go some way to meeting this criterion. The research facilitated a critical exploration of values, attitudes and beliefs by all involved through a two-way dialogue. Many strategies seemed to be significant in this respect, though I would particularly point to the use of repeated open-ended interviews, the reflection documents and 'openness' about the purposes and processes of the research.

However, such an evaluation is too simplistic as it is decontextualized: as argued above, research is constructed within a particular context. Thus the formation and maintenance of field relations have to be seen as part of the formation and maintenance of personal relationships in the daily life of Elmtree College. In overall terms, the quality of personal relationships within the college provided a receptive context for establishing the quality of field relations. Nigel Moore's (T) statement succinctly reflected the dominant ideology: 'The relationships we have here are second to none. I don't think anywhere in the city can boast the relationships we have here.' Furthermore, in some respects, the authority status of teachers had been dismantled. For instance, there was no staffroom, the dining-room and toilets were shared by staff and students, and first-name terms were used between teachers and students. This, then, provided the context for the development of some reciprocity and mutuality in field relations.

The research can also be seen as being limited in this respect by the context. The limited 'solidarity' or 'community spirit' within the college shaped the research processes with respect to a more collaborative or collective approach. The research generated little in the sense of it being planned and evaluated by the community within the college as a whole, or even by groups there. Group discussions took place by 'accident': either through informal gatherings (e.g. over lunch) or formal gatherings of students, that is, during teaching sessions. I made tentative attempts to instigate a more collaborative approach but they floundered (e.g. the suggestion that the staff could prepare an agreed statement for publication, reflecting their experiences during the first year of operation of the college).

Finally, a critique of the process of research must include the possibility that the research itself played a part in the social control of the participants. As social relationships generally within the college could be seen as a process of controlling students, so too could the research be seen as a process of controlling the participants. First, my relationships with students were established within the same hierarchical framework of teachers' relationships with students. Thus I could be said to have been a 'teacher' furthering the control of students as any other teacher at Elmtree. Secondly, the participants voiced their critique of the college, the education system and the oppression they faced. They disclosed anxieties and frustrations, sometimes venting their anger about situations they had faced and feelings of powerlessness. This process can be seen as a diverting of critique, or as a cathartic process in which 'dialogue' furthered my vested interests (in producing the thesis), and contributed to the maintenance of status quo in power relations.

Does the research promote people's prediction and control over the decision-making processes which shape their education and lives? It can be argued that this criterion was met in many ways within the research, for instance: sampling decisions were negotiated with participants; open-ended interviews could be directed by participants; and the use of reflection documents which repeatedly allowed participants to comment on analyses of their views. This perhaps emerges most clearly in the participants' responses to the reflection documents: that is, they did, in participants' eyes, accurately reflect their experiences and views. To an extent, then participants did have a say in effecting the implementation and evaluation of the research process.

However, there has also been a contrary recurring theme in participants' views and expectations. This particularly emerged in participants' views of the research as 'evaluation', that is, as a process in which they and their work were being judged. The research was seen as my responsibility, and a process which I ultimately directed and controlled. In such conceptions, the participants' perceived role was as the objects of the research. This was in part associated with general expectations about the nature of 'research', but was also consistent with aspects of the dominant ideology which justified hierarchical power relations within the college. For instance, the access to, and power within, the research was far easier for teachers than for students (and non-teaching staff).

Does the research promote people's struggles against oppression and man-made sufferings and support the removal of barriers to equal opportunities and a full participatory democracy for all? This stands as the most problematic and challenging question to apply to the research process, particularly given the perceived inequalities in access, relations and structures in a segregated institution. I would want to argue that the research was a process of identifying, documenting and discussing not only the inequalities between teachers and students but also differential access, discrimination and marginalizing of groups in society. There were signs that these discussions were taken up beyond the immediate processes of research. Adam Rose (T), for instance, took to the Staff Council the questions arising from the research concerning differential access for male and female students.

On the other hand, it can also be argued that the research effectively maintained status quo. It confirmed existing power structures, strengthened dominant ideologies and diverted critique. The research failed to establish any restructuring of services and relations which would enable democratic participation in decision-making for all, either within or beyond the college. After reading the penultimate draft of the thesis, George Goode agreed, in discussion with me, that the college 'reinforced the system'. The college would not have been allowed to exist, he argued, if it had not reinforced the system. It was an 'alternative', he maintained, but an alternative which 'points in the same direction'. Similar observations could be made about the research. If it could have challenged the system through student participation, as it aspired to, the research would not have been allowed to have been undertaken.

Concluding critical reflections

I have been left in certain respects with a 'final dilemma', and perhaps it is the contradiction which any researcher pursuing a participatory approach within special education will face. This study of student participation in decision-making was undertaken within a segregated system which in itself denies participation. I experienced this as a conflict between, on the one hand, the research furthering the 'good work' that the college was doing in the eyes of most participants and, on the other hand, engaging participants in a critical dialogue which questioned the very existence of the college as a segregated institution. This dilemma infiltrated and coloured my struggles to turn principles into practice at every stage of the research, not least in attempts to establish non-hierarchical social relations within a rigidly hierarchical context.

In essence, this was the conclusion I drew in the thesis, but in retrospect it is only part of the picture. First, there can be no such thing as a 'final dilemma' in participatory research. I now feel the need to return to the college to continue the cumulative process of analysis. In terms of participation, this 'final dilemma' is only meaningful if it generates further debate and critical dialogue between the researcher and the participants.

Secondly, the 'final dilemma' needs to be located specifically in the context of special educational needs. I would contend that the social relations in the construction of the research directly reflected the social relations in the construction of special educational needs. The challenges I faced as a researcher in the pursuit of participation reflect those in special educational needs contexts generally. Thus the three questions for 'building evaluations' of participatory research are crucial to a critique of education:

1. Does education promote both self-realization and mutual understanding through dialogue?
2. Does education promote people's prediction and control over the decision-making processes which shape their education and lives?
3. Does education promote people's struggles against oppression and man-made sufferings and support the removal of barriers to equal opportunities and a full participatory democracy for all?

Thirdly, the problematic nature of participatory research needs to be continually re-emphasized. The danger is that 'participatory' will be one of those liberal terms (such as empowerment and collaborative) which can be used as a cover for research processes which essentially promote and justify social oppression. I remain unsure in what sense the research at Elmtree could unequivocally be called 'participatory' except in 'good intentions'. But I would also suggest that it is a misconception to think of 'participatory' as a type of category of research which is either achieved or not. Earlier I quoted Lather (1986): 'journey into uncharted territory.' I have come to believe that each new research project I am involved in will be a new journey into uncharted territory and I can only hope to become a better traveller.

I end by reaffirming beliefs that have only been strengthened by my experiences at Elmtree and as a researcher. Participatory research is for me, by its nature, change-orientated research. It is research which respects and promotes the values, personal resources and capacity for self-determination of the participants in generating change. It does so in the face of power relations and structures (within both special educational needs contexts and the research processes themselves) which deny participants a say in the decision-making processes of change. However, if research is not constructed through participation it will confirm rather than challenge existing social constructions of special educational needs.

REFERENCES

Atkinson, D. and Shakespeare, P. (1993) 'Introduction', in P. Shakespeare, D. Atkinson and S. French (eds) *Reflecting on Research*. Open University Press, Milton Keynes.

Barton, L. (1988) 'Research and practice: the need for alternative perspectives', in L. Barton (ed.) *The Politics of Special Educational Needs*. Falmer Press, Lewes.

Burgess, R. G. (1984) *In the Field: an Introduction to Field Research*. Allen and Unwin, London.

Carr, W. and Kemmis, S. (1986) *Becoming Critical: Education, Knowledge and Action Research*. Falmer Press, Lewes.

Comstock, D. E. (1982) 'A method for critical research', in E. Bredo and W. Feinberg (eds) *Knowledge and Values in Social and Educational Research*. Temple University Press, Philadelphia, Pa.

Corrie, M. and Zaklukiewicz, S. (1985) 'Qualitative research and case study approaches: an introduction', in S. Hegarty and P. Evans (eds) *Research and Educational Methods in Special Education*. NFER-Nelson, Windsor.

French, S. (1993) *Practical Research: A Guide for Therapists*. Butterworth-Heinemann, Oxford.

Giroux, H. A. (1983) *Theory and Resistance in Education: A Pedagogy for the Opposition*. Heinemann, London.

Hall, B. L. (1981) 'The democratization of research in adult and non-formal education', in P. Reason and J. Rowan (eds) *Human Inquiry: A Sourcebook of New Paradigm Research*. Wiley, Chichester.

Lather, P. (1986) 'Research as praxis', *Harvard Educational Research*, Vol. 56, no. 3, pp. 257–77.

Oliver, M. (1992) 'Changing the social relations of research production?', *Disability, Handicap and Society*, Vol. 7, no. 2, pp. 101–14.

Reason, P. and Heron, J. (1986) 'Research with people: the paradigm of cooperative experiential inquiry', *Person-Centered Review*, Vol. 1, no. 4, pp. 456–76.

Rogers, C. (1978) *Carl Rogers on Personal Power: Inner Strength and its Revolutionary Impact*. Constable, London.

Shakespeare, P. (1993) 'Performing', in P. Shakespeare, D. Atkinson and S. French (eds) *Reflecting On Research*. Open University Press, Milton Keynes.

Swain, J. (1993) 'A vocational special college: preparing students for a participatory democracy?', *Disability, Handicap and Society*, Vol. 8, no. 3, pp. 293–307.

Tripp, D. H. (1983) 'Co-authorship and negotiation: the interview as an act of creation', *Interchange*, Vol. 14, no. 3, pp. 32–45.

Woods, P. (1986) *Inside Schools: Ethnography in Educational Research*. Routledge & Kegan Paul, London.

Zarb, G. (1992) 'On the road to Damascus: first steps towards changing the relations of disability research production', *Disability, Handicap and Society*, Vol. 7, no. 2, pp. 125–38.

7

ENTERING THE UNKNOWN: CASE-STUDY ANALYSIS IN SPECIAL SCHOOLS

John Hill

In making a contribution to the development of a sociology of special education, case-study research I undertook (Hill, 1992), attempted to raise issues that are central to a critical analysis of special schooling. In doing this a key motivation was to help uncover an area of schooling that, despite being a principal feature of the state education system, had little in terms of documentation except in the descriptive sense. The aim of this review is to document specific aspects of that research and to offer some explanation of the assumptions, understandings and conflicts that helped to determine its outcome. In detailing issues raised as part of the case-study analyses there will be an implicit understanding that the ideal model of a succinctly planned and precisely executed research programme is largely 'an idealised conception' (Walford, 1991, p. 1), and that engagement in long-term analysis is a social process which is both determined by and determining of the events under review. In presenting what is essentially a personal account, therefore, documentation will be descriptive and self-critical and will make reference to both theoretical and methodological issues.

THE RESEARCH: AN OVERVIEW

During the period September 1987–July 1992, I conducted research which was ultimately to lead to a PhD (Hill, 1992). The case-study analysis undertaken was ethnographic and, using sociological perspectives as an underlying base, sought to penetrate the social world of the special school. As the project unfolded, and for ease of organization and understanding, the research was divided into three parts. Part 1 described the sociohistoric context of special education. It also presented an overview of the relationship between special education and sociological theory. Part 2 concerned the case studies which took place in two special schools, each in different local authorities. Part 3 arose out of the investigation in Part 2, and provided an analysis of gender within the statementing processes of the two local authorities.

The focus of this chapter will centre on Part 2 of the study and will seek to give an account of the way the case studies developed. This will involve a discussion of the general principles and processes that underlie the research, and will also make reference to the influences, suppositions, contradictions and tensions that unfolded within the collection of data. As a basis to this evaluation, therefore, it is necessary to outline the background and major theme of the project as a whole and to offer some explanation of how the analysis was generated.

Thus my research interests were, and are, located within the area of special education. Academically they are a reflection both of theoretical debate via an MA in sociology and of school-focused research via secondment to a special needs diploma. Practically, such interests helped me as a practising teacher to understand the difficulties I encountered coping with the established psychological perspectives surrounding special education. They also led me to place developments that had occurred during my teaching career, e.g. the Warnock Report (DES, 1978) and the Education Act 1981 (HMSO, 1981), within a perspective that took account of the wider socioeconomic and political context of education as a whole. The result of such considerations was the development of a more critical approach to special education and to an acceptance of the need to move away from individualistic perspectives. It was also to lead to an increased reliance both on established sociological insights within educational theory in general and the growing sociological involvement with concepts surrounding special education.

While the result of such considerations clearly had an effect on my understandings, the decision to pursue further research and, equally important, the direction it would take, was not an easy task. Thus professionally I had an ideological commitment to special education (i.e. that was my job). I also felt that, despite looking from 'within', I could engage in a critical assessment of the ideology and patterns of educational provision in the area. What did concern me, however (and was ultimately the deciding factor in pursuing research in this area), was that my experience and understandings of special education as a whole were marginal in that my knowledge did not extend to those places where the vast majority of statemented children were educated, namely the special school. In this way there appeared to be (though still somewhat vague) a perception on my behalf that there were two kinds of special education, i.e. that which existed on the margins of mainstream and was mainly dependent for its status on the ideology of the school and staff as a whole, and that which existed within special schools where the sole purpose and ideology (and hence status) surrounded the education of children who had been separated from mainstream. In other words, plans to enter such institutions was, at least initially for me, a step into a world where a presumed 'real' special education occurred. Indeed, implicit in this perception was the view that special schooling for the most part engendered its own structure, culture and ideology and that membership of it meant entering a social world that was clearly different from the rest of the educational system. Research for me therefore meant an acceptance of this fact and my efforts were put into gaining entry and making sense of what I saw. In this sense the notion of special schooling as an entity was paramount to my thinking. A first step, and one that it is necessary briefly to share, is some perspective about the purpose and form of special schools.

OUTLINING THE ISSUE:
WHAT DO WE MEAN BY SPECIAL SCHOOLS?

Special schools, as educational institutions, were initially established during the nineteenth century and expanded alongside mainstream provision. Their number (in England and Wales) nearly doubled in the period 1945–71, rising from 528 to 1,019 (Jowett, Hegarty and Moses, 1988), and again increased rapidly following the transfer of the mentally handicapped from health to education in 1971, e.g. between 1971 and 1972 (including hospital schools) an additional 482 special schools or special establishments were made available, catering for an additional 26,833 pupils (DES, 1975). Since that period the number of special schools has remained fairly static. Thus figures for 1990 (DES) show that (in England), including hospital schools, there were 1,397 special schools with a pupil population of 97,141 and a teaching force of 16,401.

Within such schools there has been, over time, a generally agreed consensus about the treatment of children in attendance, which, as Pritchard (1963, p. 215) suggested, means '. . . a slow pace, a secure environment and an education based on the practical needs of children of low intellectual ability'. The DES (1965) supported this view, noting that a child required special schooling if he or she needed, for his or her proper progress and development, something more specialized than an ordinary school could provide. That something they suggested meant embracing '. . . the whole emotional, physical as well as the intellectual life of the child' (ibid., p. 15). Guilliford (1971, p. 10) indeed highlights the point that the special school can offer '. . . clearly defined aims and a well-planned progression of education in all its aspects, including preparation for and supervision of transition to working life'. Brennan (1971) further promotes such beliefs and, writing during the period of rapid special-school expansion, points out what he considers to be the dangers of allowing special-school children to be integrated into mainstream. In particular he notes that teachers in mainstream may lack either the skill or experience to deal with 'remedial' children and, as a result, '. . . the backward child who does not enter a special school is left in the most hazardous situation in the whole education system' (ibid., p. 11). Finally, Cole (1990, p. 105), in a more recent review, concludes that there has been a generally accepted view that children with special needs are best taught '. . . in classes containing children with similar problems and of a similar age, in schools staffed by professionals with experience of their client group'.

Such commentary, therefore, while pointing to the relative isolation of special schools, also highlights what are seen as their essential strengths. As Fish (1984, p. 10) points out, '. . . the active, thoughtful, well run special school can be a major resource centre for the groups of special educational needs it is set up to meet. It can develop methods and materials. Above all it can provide a setting in which an individual's special educational needs can be met'. Clearly, such descriptions are not without foundation, relying heavily on a humanistic perspective of special schooling. Indeed such a theme is central to the history of special education.

A critical response to such descriptions, however, highlights a less favourable outlook. Jowett, Hegarty and Moses (1988, p. 141), for example, question the role of special schools in providing an alternative to mainstream, noting that they '. . . face the danger of becoming irrelevant, continuing in existence only because of inertia and the difficulty in finding a better alternative'. Dessent (1989, p. 95), moreover, questions the basis on which special schools are maintained, noting that 'The tendency to segregate responsibility for children with special needs is both cause and effect of a segregated special education system. The tendency is maintained by the fact that advisory, administrative and financial segregation also occurs in most local Education Authorities'. Thomas (1992) reinforces this point and also notes that there is a clear mutual interest among schools, bureaucrats and professionals in maintaining the separation between mainstream and special. Indeed, Swann (1985), Jowett, Hegarty and Moses (1988) and Berliner (1991) have all highlighted the relatively small movement of pupils and teachers between these different educational sectors. Finally, Sewell (1982, p. 1), in making a critical analysis of the traditional basis of remedial education (and hence its application to special schooling), characterizes the role of the pupil '. . . as a deficit system and the teacher as an expert who diagnosed his wants and prescribed for them'.

Such interpretations clearly highlight a variance of views. They also distinguished for me the struggle between those who looked at special schooling from a management perspective and those who looked at it from a critical perspective. What clearly emerged in this review stage therefore was a view that, while there was much to be applauded within special schooling, there was an increasing body of knowledge that was critical towards them.

Moreover, while recognizing that in order to survive many had adapted, the central point remained that special schooling provides 'something different' and that the basis of this is dependent on an understanding of the type of pupil in attendance. Indeed, it was the acceptance of this 'perceived difference' which made valid contributions not only to a body of knowledge surrounding special schooling but also to the essentials of making a critical appraisal of what goes on within them.

In attempting to develop such insights, however, it is evidence, as Mittler (1985) notes, that there is little to build on in that, despite the attention given to complex issues within mainstream schools, research into special schools has been scarce. Moreover, the dominant theme within such analyses has been functional, offering documentation rather than explanation. Goode (1984, p. 228), for example, notes that '. . . the vast majority of papers in the field have been either clinical or experimental, relying almost exclusively upon "scientific" procedures such as hypothesis testing; statistical analysis of data; theory building and the like'. An acknowledgement of such perspectives thus highlights the way 'special needs' children are perceived and managed and promotes the view that the 'right resources' and 'professional teamwork' is the best way forward (Tomlinson, 1989, p. 415). Implicit in such criticism, however, is the acceptance that there are alternative approaches. Corrie and Zakluliewicz (1985, p. 124) thus suggest that there is a need to move away from 'hard facts' and 'practical implications' and, rather, they propose, that '. . . a greater use of qualitative studies would allow a sufficiently detailed and accurate picture of the processes of special education to be built up'. Mittler (1985, p. 72) also presents the view that what is needed are '. . . organisational studies that will throw light on the changing role of special schools . . . and . . . detailed studies of the special school itself'.

In summary, therefore, a key in searching for ways forward when looking at special schooling lay, for me, not only within the critical response to their perceived role but also in the search for a challenging and meaningful research analysis. In other words, after accepting the reality of special schooling and anticipating its nature and substance, the central concern became one of generating the type of theory and methods that I could rely on. Importantly it also meant engaging in an analysis that presented the issue within a sociological context. Clearly there was never any doubt that the research could be approached from any other position (bearing in mind my background and interests within the discipline). However difficulties did present themselves and were at times hard to reconcile. Chief among these was the level at which analysis could be approached.

HIGHLIGHTING A PERSPECTIVE

Hargreaves (1985, p. 23), in defining this difficulty, presents the choice faced by sociologists as one of perception, i.e. between '. . . different levels of reality, between patterns of educational structure and the texture of daily life . . . between different ways of looking at reality, between interpretative and normative approaches'. For those involved in issues surrounding special education this is no less problematic. Thus a brief review of the history of special schooling highlights not only the way particular groups of children have been placed within special education (see, for example, Coard, 1971) but also how definitions of 'disability' and professional involvement in the placement and management of such groups have contributed to what may now be seen as a highly organized and bureaucratic sector of education. Sociologically therefore the use of structural and/or interactional analysis offers explanations other than the merely functional. The difficulty for this research was not only which perspective to adopt but also whether it was possible (within a case-study analysis of a school) to reconcile differences between levels of theory. A review of ways forward (see, for example, Hammersley, 1984; Adleman and Young, 1985) suggests that the latter is not an easy task. However, an adoption of a specific perspective may result not only in the acceptance of a 'paradigmatic mentality' (Quicke, 1986, p. 81) but also could contribute to the research developing around theoretical perspectives rather than substantial research problems (Hammersley, 1986).

A way out of this impasse, and one that was eventually adopted, was suggested by Hargreaves (1985, p. 170) who, under the influence of Merton's (1968) 'theory of the middle range', noted that

> . . . between the rules, negotiations and bargainings of classroom interaction, and the dynamics of the capitalist economy or the relative autonomy of the state, lie a whole range of intermediary processes and structures which have largely been neglected in sociological accounts of education; such things as 'institutional bias . . . teacher cultures . . . teacher coping strategies and so on.

In other words, what he terms the 'meso' level of analysis. Such an understanding neither rejects the view that power and conflict are key determinants within special schooling nor does it overlook the influence of those within such schools to influence events. The consequent adoption of this perspective was thus a difficult yet key decision in the research programme in that it not only gave me a base from which to develop but also presented an opportunity to highlight macro and microissues from what was essentially an elective position. Finally, by looking at special schools from an organizational perspective, two other factors, as highlighted by Hammersley (1990), could be fulfilled, namely, that there is a specific focus to the research and that it addresses an issue of importance. Essentially, therefore, I had found a way of working that seemed theoretically sound in that it pointed me towards an organizational analysis which also left other levels of insight open to me. In this way I had secured what I was looking for in that I had neither buried the research with guidelines that were too specific nor was I left to the vagueness of being a mere reporter. Indeed, such a way forward provided much security for me in that I had now defined a context from which to proceed.

The second major feature of the study and one that emanated from theoretical perspective adopted was the generation of a precise research programme. Thus from the organizational perspective now adopted it was possible to speculate that special schools, historically socially structured as separate institutions (from mainstream), have developed their own 'cultural determinants' which both promote and maintain their identity. The key concern of the case studies, therefore, was an attempt to distinguish and to offer explanation for and insight into these determinants. In other words the research would aim to focus not simply on the structural position of special schools nor on the minutiae of the international analysis within, but rather would concentrate on the key features of the special school that give it support as a unique type of school. In doing this it was the intention to accept the political nature underlying a separate special-school system, and also to attempt to build upon a potential substantial research area within the sociology of special education. In this way the search for internal mechanisms that defined the structure and culture of such schools now became the central focus and, in a sense, predetermined what was to follow.

DEVELOPING A METHODOLOGY

In developing research based at the level of the organization the focus of analysis was the school. Here case-study inquiry allowed for exploration of two special schools in their everyday settings using a variety of formal and informal procedures. By using case studies, therefore, as the model from which to generate information (rather than, for example, using quantitative methods over a large number of schools), it became the theme of the research to focus qualitatively on them as working institutions. In this way, as noted earlier, the central theme would operate around understanding the key processes under which they functioned as educational institutions.

Clearly, however, a working methodology is not a simplistic operation, and in this case involved an amount of compromise. Thus early in the research proposals a decision was made to use schools that were at the disparate ends of the special-school spectrum (i.e. moderate learning difficulties – MLD – and emotional and behavioural difficulties – EBD). The theory behind this was that (if my understandings were accurate) the rationale behind all special schools is similar despite any differences in appearance. However, the schools finally chosen were to a large extent a product of the LEAs who had given me consent.

This presented a great deal of concern in the sense that not only had some control been taken away from me but also that the ground was being prepared in advance. One particular concern was that the theoretical position of the research could be invalidated by the scope of access provided. In part as a reaction to this, though always central to the aims of the research, two decisions were made, namely, to be 'close to the action' – e.g. working alongside teachers, joining in staff meetings, doing supply teaching, etc., and also that it was necessary to 'come clean' at an early stage of each case study and state in as clear a way as possible the intentions of the research. Clearly this was a risk in that it could influence the relationship between myself and the staff within the school. However I viewed it necessary in order to gain access in the way required. It would also, I presumed, help those most interested to contribute to the outcome. In methodological terms this part of the research process became known as 'democratic evaluation' (see, for example, MacDonald, 1976; Walker, 1986).

As an underpin to such methodology, however, access was gained to a number of other special schools in the hope that some degree of comparison could take place (in the final documentation this became known as 'comparative analysis'). In particular, a point of focus became the EBD special school I was working in part time (while conducting the research) and specifically the head, who became important in helping to clarify detail about the structure of special schools within the local authority. Indeed it was here that I not only attempted to validate what I had begun to consider as important features of special schooling but also to look for objections to such assumptions.

COLLECTING DATA

While the early part of the research therefore was not a comfortable experience, it was not long before involvement with case-study schools became a less severe task. Indeed it is perhaps in the nature of schools to allow (to some extent) the absorption of 'outsiders' and the mere fact that I was a teacher and was 'known' by some of the staff that made the situation less of a strain than anticipated. The possibility of compliancy, however, is obvious, and the need to ask awkward and difficult questions can be made more difficult because of closeness of relationships formed in the school. In order to avoid such difficulties an urgency to document became overwhelming. In doing this the influence of Cohen and Taylor (1977) was forcibly felt. Thus in their recollections of research at Durham Jail they highlight (pp. 71–2) the moment when it became necessary to adopt more definite strategies, i.e.:

> . . . we gradually realized that some formal constraints were necessary. Up to that point we had been behaving like naive inductionists, hoping that

patterns, themes and dimensions would emerge if we talked long enough. However, it became clear that our notes on the conversations resisted any such structuring . . . We were accordingly drawn into adopting certain methodological devices in order to bring some order to our material.

Although not yet at such a stage (though with this clearly in mind and after much consideration), a decision was made at an early stage, i.e. three to four months to make public those key dimensions it was thought necessary to examine. These included:

1. a historical understanding of the development of each school;
2. the shared characteristics of the children;
3. the nature of social control;
4. approaches to teaching practices;
5. the nature of knowledge;
6. the role of management; and
7. the ideology of teachers.

At this point, however, some concern was still evident. Thus in adopting such a way forward I was acutely aware that the decision to categorize at such an early stage could lead to the charge that the research was in some way led by certain presuppositions. Clearly the influences of structuralist perspectives can be seen in formulating such understandings (and, in particular, the radical-structuralism of, for example, Sigmon, 1987; Sleeter, 1989; Tomlinson, 1989). Yet to some extent it can be justified as an inevitable result of earlier deliberations and kind of theoretical base identified. Indeed in conducting such analysis the notion of validity needs to be woven into processes which are patently not neutral (Barton, 1988) and rest to a greater or lesser degree on the values of those conducting research. Thus what became important for me was that the understandings generated were subject to review and critical analysis. Atkinson (1977, p. 32) indeed summarizes this problem when he notes that

> The range of different strategies currently available in sociology not only ensures that researchers are faced with a difficult problem of choice between alternatives, but also guarantees that whatever they choose they will lay themselves open to attack from all the other alternative positions set aside. One implication of this is that a certain amount of toughness is required if one is to make a choice.

While this 'toughness' can be seen as an excuse to pursue research without regard to criticism, there were times when events did cause a change in emphasis.

An example (case study 1) may be highlighted in the way that I was challenged by one member of staff of paying too much attention to the views of the head and being 'led' towards certain presumptions by the headteacher. As a result, and after discussion with a number of staff, I made a positive attempt to change procedure and to spend increased time working with teachers 'on the ground'. I also made a conscious effort to make more use of 'key informants' as a base from which to check assumptions. In this way the research process was reformulated.

The decision to be involved 'on the ground' did, however, cause continual difficulties. Thus most involvement did arise naturally out of the early formulation of relationships in the schools and, as suggested earlier, may be attributable to the fact that I had a working knowledge of special schooling and was less of an 'outsider'. The acceptance of my presence, however, and my general participation in the life of the schools posed problems. Indeed, at times it became difficult to be detached from events. It also meant that I was less able to 'control' my role as researcher and also to maintain objectivity.

Occasions also occurred when my role as an 'outsider' was clearly obvious – for example, although most staff appreciated 'an extra pair of hands', some made it clear, if not in words, that I was disrupting their daily routine. It was at such times that I became aware that in reality I was at the edge of what was going on. Jorgensen (1989, p. 12), in articulating this point, thus notes that 'The deeper meanings of most forms of human existence are not displayed for outsiders. They are available primarily to people for whom these meanings constitute a way of life.'

Indeed a deeper insight into the world of the special school suggests that gaining an understanding of the culture within is more of a task than with a mainstream school. Thus while all schools remain to some extent secretive and (most) teachers remain more or less protective about their personal environment, it may be suggested that the special school is unique in that its operation, for the most part, takes place in a closed world. Thus the professional identity and job expectations of mainstream (junior and secondary) teachers mediate outwards towards parents, community and an ideology that is hierarchical (i.e. based on specific stages of children's development). Conversely, the special school is dominated by an ideology that is deficit orientated and relies to a great extent on the professionalism of others, i.e. psychologists, speech therapists, social workers, doctors, etc. In this way the 'context' of the teacher role is changed and moves away from the 'academic' and more towards the 'personal' forms of education. Consequently, for the researcher the 'hidden agenda' of mainstream (i.e. the nature of teacher–pupil relationships) becomes the main focus on which special schools operate. Understanding the meanings and motives of individuals therefore becomes a difficult task, and was one that needed constant reappraisal.

Indeed, as the research professed, this notion took on a more powerful focus. In particular the emphasis on understanding the institutional context of individual actions meant constantly interpreting actions and events in a way that gave structured meaning to them. Ambiguity and misinterpretation was therefore a central issue, and led to a process (particularly in the first case-study school) whereby every effort would be made to discuss findings with staff and attempt to search out contradictory evidence.

My final methodological concern, and one that was felt throughout the research process, was that I was operating between two 'social worlds' (Quicke, 1992). Thus I became aware, as Pugh (1988) acknowledges, of the suspicion that the chief motive in conducting research is to advance the researcher's career rather than to advance knowledge. I was also aware, as Stahl (1991) observes, of the perception that most research is remote from educational practice. Finally, like Threadgold (1985, p. 252), there was concern that like others carrying out ethnographic work in schools I was defining problems '. . . with an audience of fellow researchers rather than teachers in mind'. Taken together such concerns highlighted the contradiction that, while belonging to one group (teachers), I was involved in pursuing the goal of another group (academics). The fact that the outlook, perception and, indeed, language of the two varied left me in a position that was on occasions difficult. This was to be most apparent in my first 'report back' in case study 2, where a half-hour presentation was greeted with silence and no questions! Despite such set-backs, however, meetings with my supervisors seemed to be positive, and issues raised and methodology pursued were well received. The paradox here seemed obvious and was further highlighted on reading the criticisms received by Burgess (1985, p. 104) after she presented her completed case study to the collaborating school: 'It seems ironic to me that the style of research, methods of social investigation and finalized account of my study should be held in high regard by my supervisors . . . and yet only six weeks later were highly criticized by the teachers involved in the research.'

Such concerns clearly surfaced during my initial involvement with case study 2. Thus while this may in some way reflect the difference between the two establishments being researched, it could also be a reflection of my changing outlook or reduced enthusiasm for further research. My response was to promote an increased collaborative approach whereby rather than present lengthy papers to the whole staff I attempted to engage in small-scale discussions with two or three of the staff and pursue issues with individuals. I also changed to a policy of presenting my findings verbally rather than in written form. The result of such changes in strategies certainly had an effect and took the pressure off me as a presenter of 'issues' and also the staff who were expected to respond. More specifically it meant that 'talk' with small groups led to the emergence of more critical responses and an enlivened dialogue.

In this way I had confronted what was an 'issue' to me in keeping control of the data. However it did mean that a degree of 'tactics' had been used in order to maintain structure to what I was doing. Clearly my own response had evoked increased dialogue but had done so only in the sense that it was a 'safer' way to progress. (In my first case study 'safeness' was never a concern.) There is, therefore, a case to suggest that as I gained in confidence as a research practitioner I became more adept at managing the processes involved, and also the closer I became to the academic (i.e. my supervisors and fellow researchers). Moreover, the urgency and need to write up also added sharper focus for a need to control possible outcomes. In this way drive and challenging enthusiasm in 'entering the unknown' slowly evolved from an attempt to make sense of what I saw to managing what I had seen. Though this (perhaps) did not diminish the final outcome there was a period when it felt involvement with the specifics of research had generated outcomes that were in no small part a reflection of considerations other than the original issues. In this way the 'field' of study that surrounded special schooling helped create its own destiny in a way that may be seen from the researcher's perspective as being part of a dialectical process that engulfed a range of internal and external struggles.

CONCLUSION: SPECIAL SCHOOLS AS AN AREA OF RESEARCH

In documenting research into special schooling, this chapter has sought to highlight ways in which theoretical assumptions surrounding special education were developed and used to determine both the focus and methodology of case-study analyses. An attempt has also been made to show that the case studies were conducted in what was essentially an interactive process. Evident within such research, moreover, was the assumption that the groundwork for this analysis had already been documented (albeit in different forms) by others. By looking at issues surrounding the functioning of special schooling, therefore, an attempt was made to show how they could be substantiated within an organizational analysis.

Importantly for this study, therefore, the major ingredient was the belief that the world being explored (like case studies of mainstream schools) is a social world and as such the special school is characterized by specific cultural determinants. An acceptance of this was thus central to the research as a whole and helped create the 'field' in which to operate. Consequently the sociological investigation undertaken, rather than being descriptive, attempted to present critical analysis both of the appearance and reality of what went on within.

What was gained from the analysis was some understanding (however limited) of a world that has generally been taken for granted. Indeed, while sociological insight has focused on aspects of the social world of mainstream schools (see, for example, Hargreaves, 1984) for reasons that may be attributed to the status of research in this area (see, for example, Quicke, 1984; Oliver, 1985), special schools have escaped detailed ethnographic scrutiny. What may also be witnessed is the way that the analysis has made an attempt to distance itself from particular issues that currently dominated debate within the area. Thus it was always my acceptance that notions of, for example, increased 'integration' or 'collaboration' redefining statementing procedure or promoting access to the National Curriculum were arguments that were marginal to the central debate. Clearly this was a rejection of a perspective that added to the management and organizational approach to special schooling. Moreover there is more than an implicit understanding that such a rejection also takes task with the more generalized forms of psychological/medical assumptions that have dominated the field.

While being clear therefore of the type of ethnographic investigation necessary to focus on the culture and structure of special schools, there was also a sense that there was an audience to reach. Thus echoing Dessent's (1989, p. 233) call for '. . . a need for greater openness and frank discussion about the issues which currently impinge upon the special school', a central feature of my thought was towards those who were on the receiving end of such a system. By looking at outcomes of what children received, for example, what kind of knowledge, what kind of ideology, what kind of control, I was better able to come to terms with what was important in maintaining the essential supports of such education. Moreover in doing so there was an appeal not only to those 'professionals' who have power within special education but also a focus on issues that the community of parents and pupils could identify with.

For those who may also wish to detail the social world of the special school, therefore, the essence of my own research within case-study analysis has been to look critically at the internal features which support and maintain them as unique institutions. That the outcome was specific (i.e. it outlined particular support mechanisms) meant that essentially what had been presented was an 'ideal model'. That such a model can be criticized is clearly apparent (as can all small-scale ethnographic research) in that what has been perceived could be seen as both highly selective and specific to those institutions under review. What was more important, however, was that the rationale that generated the research had created the context from which to proceed. In this way for this researcher the theoretical approach was as equally important in searching for ways forward in the 'field' as the outcomes it created.

REFERENCES

Adelman, C. and Young, M. F. D. (1985) 'The assumptions of educational research. The last twenty years in Great Britain', in M. Shipman (ed.) *Educational Research: Principles, Policies and Practices*. Harper & Row, London.

Atkinson, M. (1977) 'Coroners and the categorisation of deaths as suicides. Changes in perspective as features of the research process', in C. Bell and H. Newby (eds) *Doing Sociological Research*. Allen & Unwin, London.

Barton, L. (1988) 'Research and practice. The need for alternative perspectives', in L. Barton (ed.) *The Politics of Special Educational Needs*. Falmer Press, Lewes.

Berliner, W. (1991) 'The outsiders still left in the cold', *Educational Guardian*, 10 December.

Brennan, W. K. (1971) 'A policy for remedial education', *Remedial Education*, Vol. 6, no. 1, pp. 7–11.

Burgess, H. (1985) 'Case study and curriculum research: some issues for teacher researchers', in R. G. Burgess (ed.) *Issues in Educational Research*. Falmer Press, Lewes.

Coard, B. (1971) *How the West Indian Child is Made Educationally Subnormal in the British School System*. New Beacon Press, London.

Cohen, S. and Taylor, L. (1977) 'Talking about prison blues', in C. Bell and H. Newby (eds) *Doing Sociological Research*. Allen & Unwin, London.

Cole, T. (1990) 'The history of special education: social control or humanitarian progress?', *British Journey of Special Education*, Vol. 17, no. 3, pp. 107–17 (research supplement).

Corrie, S. and Zaklukiewicz, S. (1985) 'Qualitative research and case-study approaches: an introduction', in S. Hegarty and P. Evans (eds) *Research and Evaluation Methods in Special Education*. NFER/Nelson, Slough.

DES (1965) *Reports on Education, Special Education Today*, no. 23, July. HMSO, London.

DES (1975) *Statistics of Education, Vol. 1: Schools*. HMSO, London.

DES (1978) *Special Educational Needs. Report of the Committee of Enquiry into the Education of Handicapped Children and Young People* (Warnock Report). HMSO, London.

DES (1990) *Statistics of Education, Schools*. HMSO, London.

Dessent, T. (1978) 'The historical development of school psychological services', in B. Gillham (ed.) *Reconstructing Educational Psychology*. Croom Helm, Beckenham.

Dessent, T. (1989) 'The paradox of the special school', in D. Baker and K. Bovair (eds) *Making the Special Schools Ordinary*. Falmer Press, Lewes.

Fish, J. (1984) 'The future of the special school', in T. Bowers (ed.) *Management and the Special School*. Croom Helm, Beckenham.

Goode, D. (1984) 'Socially produced identities, intimacy and the problem of competence among the retarded', in L. Barton and S. Tomlinson (eds) *Special Education and Social Interests*. Croom Helm, Beckenham.

Guilliford, R. (1971) *Special Educational Needs*. Routledge & Kegan Paul, London.

Hammersley, M. (1984) 'The paradigmatic mentality: a diagnosis', in L. Barton and S. Walker (eds) *Social Crisis and Educational Research*. Croom Helm, Beckenham.

Hammersley, M. (1986) *Some Reflections upon the Macro-Micro Problem in the Sociology of Education*. Open University Press, Milton Keynes.

Hammersley, M. (1990) *Classroom Ethnography*. Open University Press, Milton Keynes.

Hargreaves, A. (1985) 'The micro-macro problem in the sociology of education', in R. G. Burgess (ed.) *Issues in Educational Research*. Falmer Press, Lewes.

Hargreaves, A. and Woods, P. (1984) *Classrooms and Staffrooms. The Sociology of Teachers and Teaching*. Open University Press, Milton Keynes.

Hill, J. (1991) 'Special schooling, statementing procedures and gender: a sociological case study analysis.' Unpublished PhD, Sheffield Hallam University.

HMSO (1981) *Education Act*. HMSO, London.

Jorgensen, D. L. (1989) *Participant Observation. A Methodology for Human Studies*. Sage, London.

Jowett, S., Hegart, S. and Moses, D. (1988) *Joining Forces*. NFER/Nelson, Slough.

MacDonald, B. (1976) 'Evaluation and the control of education', in D. Tawney (ed.) *Curriculum Evaluation Today: Trends and Implications*. Macmillan, London and Basingstoke.

MacDonald, M. (1981) 'Schooling and reproduction of class and gender relations', in R. Dale, G. Esland and M. MacDonald (eds) *Educational and the State*, Vol. 12. Falmer Press, Lewes.

Measor, L. and Woods, P. (1991) 'Breakthroughs and blockages in ethnographic research: contrasting experiences during the Change in Schools Project', in G. Walford (ed.) *Doing Educational Research*. Routledge, London.

Merton, R. K. (1968) *Social Theory and Social Structure*. Free Press, New York.

Mittler, P. (1985) 'Approaches to evaluation in special education: concluding reflections', in S. Hegarty and P. Evans (eds) *Research and Evaluation Methods in Special Education*. NFER/Nelson, Slough.

Oliver, M. (1985) 'The Integration–Segregation Debate: some sociological considerations', *British Journal of Sociology of Education*, Vol. 6, no. 1, pp. 75–92.

Pritchard, D. G. (1963) *Education and Handicapped 1760–1960*. Routledge & Kegan Paul, London.

Pugh, R. (1988) 'The faculty of education: people centered or paper centered?', *New Education*, Vol. 10, pp. 48–53.

Quicke, J. (1984) 'The role of the educational psychologist in the post-Warnock era', in L. Barton and S. Tomlinson (eds) *Special Education and Social Interests*. Croom Helm, Beckenham.

Quicke, J. (1986) 'A case of paradigmatic mentality? A reply to Mike Oliver', *British Journal of Sociology of Education*, Vol. 17, no. 1, pp. 81–6.

Quicke, J. (1992) 'Liberal irony and reflective teaching: a role for academic courses in in-service teacher education', *Curriculum Studies*, Vol. 24, no. 4, pp. 315–25.

Sewell, G. (1982) *Reshaping Remedial Education*. Croom Helm, Beckenham.

Sigmon, S. B. (1987) *Radical Analysis of Special Education*. Falmer Press, Lewes.

Sleeter, C. (1989) 'Using the radical structuralist paradigm to examine the creation and use of learning difficulties.' Paper presented at the Annual Convention of the Council for Exceptional Children, San Francisco, Calif., April.

Stahl, A. (1991) 'Bridging the gap between research and teacher education: an Israeli innovation', *Journal of Education for Teaching*, Vol. 17, no. 3, pp. 293–9.

Swann, W. (1985) 'Is the integration of children with special needs happening? An analysis of recent statistics of pupils in special schools', *Oxford Review of Education*, Vol. 11, no. 1, pp. 3–18.

Thomas, G. (1992) 'Local authorities, special needs and the status quo', *Support for Learning*, Vol. 7, no. 1, pp. 36–40.

Threadgold, M. (1985) 'Bridging the gap between teachers and researchers', in R. Burgess (ed.) *Issues in Educational Research*. Falmer Press, Lewes.

Tomlinson, S. (1981) *Educational Subnormality: A Study in Decision Making*. Routledge, London.

Tomlinson S. (1989) 'The radical-structuralist paradigm: unpopular perspectives in the origins and development of special education.' Paper presented at the Annual Convention of the Council for Exceptional Children, San Francisco, Calif., April.

Walford, G. (1991) *Doing Educational Research*. Routledge, London.

Walker, R. (1986) 'The conduct of educational case studies, ethics, theory and procedures', in M. Hammersley (ed.) *Controversies in Classroom Research*. Open University Press, Milton Keynes.

8

IMAGES AND THE CONSTRUCTION OF IDENTITIES IN A RESEARCH CONTEXT

Anastasia Vlachou

The main interest of the research that I am involved with is to explore teachers' and peers' attitudes towards the integration of students with Down's syndrome. Reflecting on this topic from a personal perspective, there were certain factors and accumulated experiences and knowledge that prompted me to focus my attention on attitudes and integration of disabled people.

During my early socialization process, the social dimension of disability was embraced by feelings of guilt and embarrassment. It was a life occurrence that was better hidden. Disabled children were not neighbourhood children. Whenever, accidentally, they happened to be 'visible' they were targets of curiosity, pity and fear, or they were targets of jokes. My first interactions with a person with Down's syndrome, at the age of 15, were not the same as those that took place with non-disabled people. However, it was striking at the time to figure out that the image and identity that I had constructed for a disabled person was misleading. Some years later, this experience forced me to ask: 'How, even though I had not any lived interactions with disabled people prior to the one I referred above, had I constructed a mental and a social identity of a disabled person?' Obviously the sources of obtaining information about disability issues had not derived from disabled people. The messages I was absorbing as a child originated from other able-bodied persons via social institutions such as family, church, schools and media, to name some.

Media here are of a significant importance. If for a moment we reflect on our everyday environment we realize that we are living in a visual society with mass media dominating not only our reality but also the images of this reality.

Photography is one of the many visual mechanisms that project and transmit information about the world around us.

I became interested in photography not as a photographer but as a researcher trying to explore children's images, perceptions and feelings towards their disabled peers. The decision to use a photograph was based strongly on the assumption that photographs reveal mechanisms that lead us to the formation and internalization of 'individual' needs, concepts, values and images. They include questions of interpretation, meaning and communication. They '. . . encompass the social practices, institutions and norms of a culture, providing information and expression that cannot be separated from our interpretation of any image' (English, 1981, pp. 12–13).

However, during the initial phase of deciding to use a picture as a methodological tool I had not realized how many complex issues were included in the analysis of the role of photography in relation to the social construction of what we perceive as natural and normal. In the same manner I had not realized that the social constructs and values that we as researchers bring or develop during the research process are important determinants of the way we approach and interpret the social phenomena that we endeavour to explore. For instance, my developed belief that disability is a product of the social response to individuals with an impairment not only influenced the selection of the methods but is also inevitably present in the way I conceived the topic under investigation.

Moreover, I realized that in educational attitudinal research there has been surprisingly little systematic evidence of the fact that the very methodological procedures of using a photograph constitute the topic directly. For instance, a bulk of previous research has been conducted by presenting disabled and non-disabled persons either on pictures or on videotapes in order to measure children's and teachers' attitudes towards disabled peers/students (Gottlieb, 1974; Siperstein, Gottlieb and Bak, 1976; Kennedy and Thurman, 1982; Aloia and MacMillan, 1983; Bak and Siperstein, 1986; Siperstein, Bak and O'Keefe, 1988). Even though the above studies contribute to efforts to understand some factors influencing the formation of attitudes, researchers have used their methodological tools as self-justified, taken-for-granted objective techniques which lead to the discovery of truth. No trials or errors, no double paradoxical functions; no relationships between the images presented on pictures and videotapes and the social systems which had created and used these images; no connections between the producers, the users and the products or the way that these connections influence both the researcher and the researched in producing interpretations. For instance, what does the selection of a picture which portrays '. . . an academically incompetent abnormal-appearing child' (Siperstein, Gottlieb and Bak, 1976) indicate about the ideological position of the researcher with regards to notions of normalcy and disability?

Thus I was desperately searching for other researchers' experiences that would offer me the opportunity to share the dilemmas included in the intersubjective realities that we create by using different methodological/ ideological means in approaching social issues.

The message I took from conventional attitudinal research was that in order to be valid the method has to be taken as an axiomatic technique to be used in a neutral standardized way by neutral researchers, so as to be objective and hence 'scientific'. This stereotype of a researcher who is detached and above the environment he or she tries to understand was contradicting my experience in which most decisions were based on trial, errors and reconstructions. Among other processes, the decision of using a photograph for exploring attitudes offered me the opportunity to realize how subjective and value laden both the researcher and the techniques can be. The use of photography was conceived during the time I was in the field and not prior to it. Thus strategies for using photographs were devised at the place of action and errors were unavoidable. It was the experience of errors and the search for alternative ways that helped me to realize that

> . . . to keep our options secret, to conceal them in the cobwebs of technique, or to disguise them by claiming neutrality does not constitute neutrality . . . It's naive to consider our role as abstract in a matrix of neutral methods and techniques for action that doesn't take place in a neutral society.
>
> (Freire, 1985, p. 39)

Moreover, the evolution of my ideological assumptions regarding disability, the questions I was raising and the field constraints demanded an evolution of the techniques I was using for collecting research materials. In turn, such an evolution means that the method must be constantly scrutinized and not '. . . once accepted then to be taken for granted' (Delamont and Hamilton, 1993, p. 30).

The very method itself, the photograph, the way I used it, the context in which I used it, and the stories by which it was accompanied raised complex issues so that, in order to come to terms with them, I had to place my technique in a sociohistorical and cultural spectrum.

Thus what I am concerned with here is to share some of the theoretical and practical implications that emerged from using a photograph of a disabled person for research purposes. What follows is an attempt to get to grips with the social function of photography, its relation to the production of images and, in turn, its effect on our construction of disability interpretations. Further, the main methodological dilemmas that I faced by using a photograph are going to be presented in an analysis of 1) issues concerning the selection of the photograph; 2) the rationale of using a photograph as a methodological tool; and 3) issues for consideration emerging from the paradoxical function of photographs in a research context. Before exploring the above issues it is necessary to refer briefly to the theoretical and practical framework of the study.

THEORETICAL AND PRACTICAL FRAMEWORK
OF THE STUDY

One of the initial purposes of the study was to explore children's attitudes towards their peers with Down's syndrome. During the pilot study I realized that attitudes are very difficult to define not only theoretically but also operationally. Exploring attitudes is a complicated affair as we try to find out social influences, constructs and processes that have been so much internalized by a person that they are often at the level of subconsciousness.

After some group discussions with the children and participant observations it came across that children were engaged in a web of interactions revealing a complicated culture full of feelings, emerging beliefs and values. Interactions included clusters of commonalities and differences, categorizations and prejudices, likes and dislikes, images, actual and virtual identities (in the way the terms are being defined by Goffman in *Stigma*, 1976, pp. 12–13). As Gotmann puts it metaphorically, '. . . children when beginning to make friendships must co-ordinate their efforts with all the virtuosity of an accomplished jazz quartet' (cited in Besag, 1989, p. 76).

Offering a definition of friendship is of limited value. Friendship means different things to different people, and this became one of the objectives of the study: to explore the way children perceive their interactions with other children, the way they conceive their friendships. This then would be related to the ultimate aim of the study: to explore the way they conceive their interactions and friendships with their disabled peers.

I do recognize that I draw a subtle distinction between friendship among non-disabled children and friendship between disabled and non-disabled children. Some authors have based their approach to friendship among disabled and non-disabled people on the principle that '. . . the way relationships are made, sustained and broken is no different for people with learning disabilities than they are for those without such disabilities' (Firth and Rapley, 1990, p. 27). But if that was the case in everyday life and if we (the able-bodied-minded people) had recognized that disabled people are no different in the way they conceive interactions and friendships there would not have been a need for this research.

In a great many social contexts, '. . . people who are disabled do seem to suffer a measure of social ostracism' (Thomas, 1982, p. 3) and social isolation. Interactions between non-disabled and disabled persons seem to encompass processes that are not always the same as the processes that take place within social/personal encounters among non-disabled persons.

From my experience of trying to explore the way children perceived their interactions between themselves and their peers with Down's syndrome, I realized that the researcher as an outsider of the children's world can be always on the edge of confusion. It is not only that disability issues have been transferred as a taboo to the children but it is also the issue of the representation of the self. That is, children have their own defence mechanisms to protect themselves by presenting a social desirable self to an adult (researcher). For these reasons I approached the exploration of interactions with disabled people in an indirect way.

First, I discussed with the children their perceptions of friendship in general. Secondly, I discussed with them their perceptions about their actual friends. Thirdly, I introduced a picture of two girls, one of whom had Down's syndrome. Both girls were strangers to the children. In this way I tried to explore the way they made sense of what they were seeing. What questions and answers did the picture raise for them? How did they perceive an 'ordinary non-disabled female stranger', an 'ordinary female stranger with Down's syndrome' and 'the interaction among them'?

Thus the issues of this chapter emerged from 34 group discussions, based on friendship patterns, involving 103 children (51 girls and 52 boys), with an age-range from 5:10 to 11:6. Triangular 'techniques' complemented the group discussions as I was interested in exploring aspects of the children's culture and the educational environment in which they were participating. Since I am a non-British citizen I approached each situation, in and outside the classroom, from a cultural-anthropological stance; that is, questioning what for other people who have grown up in this specific culture seemed to be unquestionable. This cultural-anthropological stance enabled me to acknowledge the cultural relativity of my society (Greek-Canadian) and of British society, while at the same time it urged me '. . . to look with renewed attention at the details which make up the "natural" attitudes of everyday life' (Webster, 1980, p. 47).

Extensive participant observations – over a year and a half – and familiarity with the children proved to be significant for my understanding of both the information I was receiving and the context to which this information was related. Moreover, prior to the group discussions, individual discussions with each of the 103 children had taken place in an effort to approach each child initially as an individual, to build rapport with them and to offer them the opportunity of choice in case they would not like to participate in the group discussions. These individual discussions served as the basis for the creation of the atmosphere and the questions asked during the group discussions. Finally, interviews with teachers, who constantly encountered students in a variety of everyday situations, took place in an effort to explore their philosophy of education, their opinions, suggestions and anxieties regarding both educational practices and the implementation of integration policies.

My theoretical-ideological orientation with regard to the function of photographs has influenced the practices of this study and before presenting the methodological dilemmas of using a photograph in this research context it is important to present my perspective of the social function of this visual communicative material.

SETTING THE PERSPECTIVE

We do believe that photographers are already in politics. This is because the images we make carry ideological messages which, cumulatively, help to shape people's ideas, values and attitudes. If we are shown enough pictures of women's bodies or packets of Daz, then we could probably conclude that society has a value for such imagery. Equally, if we don't see certain aspects of society then we could conclude that their omission (if we even notice it) is because they are of no importance. In this respect photographers cannot be anything but political.

(Dennell, T. and Spence, J. 'The Unpolitical Photograph?', in Webster, 1980, p. 146)

Since the day that the camera was invented photographs, in addition to their aesthetic value, both then and now have been used as a powerful means of non-verbal communication. They project in a persuasive manner images, ideas and information in order to influence people's attitudes or even to control their reactions towards different social phenomena. It is not coincidental that '. . . soon after the development of the camera all types of groups ranging from the representatives of the government to business leaders sought to exploit it in deliberate endeavors to influence the attitudes and the actions of . . . viewers' (English, 1981, p. 1).

The questions then emerge: 'What are the sources from which this technological device draws its persuasive power?' and 'If photographs are so political, why the prevailing myth that they are apolitical?' How can we explain the paradoxes that the use of photography encompasses, such that photography has apparently no language of its own but it has been used extensively for communicative purposes. In itself the photograph cannot lie but it has been used to deceive and misinform. Compared with other means of communication it is weak in intentionality but this weakness is its greater strength (Berger and Mohr, 1982, pp. 90–7). Any analysis of the above questions and ambiguities can be achieved only if *a photograph can be perceived as a means of expression in a social system in which history, culture, communication and power relationships are being inextricably connected.*

One attraction of the photograph for humans has always been the capacity to freeze and capture an event in time by using a technological product. As English (1981, p. 6) stated: '. . . although a person or event faded into history, its image remained to be viewed again and again, which kept precious memories alive and prevented their unique poignancy from diminishing with the passage of time.' Capturing the time is highly connected with memories. In turn memories are alive in references to images of the lived experience. Every story and meaning accompanying the picture encompasses the dimension of subjectivity, a dimension that is not highly recognized when related to technological advances.

However, simultaneously another source of photography's appeal has been connected with its use in scientific inquiry. This second use of photography was highly appreciated as it produced material benefits. The overestimation of the technological scientific utility of photography can be understood in relation to the historical-ideological systems in which the photographic production was developed. English (ibid., p. 10) inform us that '. . . the material benefits of applied photography were enthusiastically received because the medium at its most fundamental level was also in perfect harmony with the dominant intellectual current of the time: Positivism'. He goes further (ibid.) by explaining that the prevailing belief was that '. . . the camera simply recorded reality and provided factual evidence, conforming with the positivist concern to objectify nature into a system of observable phenomena capable of empirical investigation'. Thus the photographic production became an apolitical, technological, objective means of transferring information. In such an ideological framework subjectivity was imparted from the uses of the tool, even when sociopolitical agencies started to exploit the potential of this tool. Since the images and events presented by photography were highly associated with the 'true representation of reality' the main political function of photography '. . . would be to communicate pure information that visualized a limitless number of subjects and themes' (ibid., p. 12). It was the establishment of this myth that helped social agencies to transmit highly cultural, subjective and political messages as objective and true. In reinforcing this myth, the photographic production uses highly sophisticated, controlled and selective mechanisms which often aim to be received with little reflection.

What has not been distinguished is the different levels of truth that photographic production include according to the context in which they have been used. Berger and Mohr (1982, p. 98, emphasis added) offer this distinction between the three different uses of photography, and consequently different levels of the truth they reveal. They claim:

> . . . in fact, when a photograph is used scientifically, its unquestionable evidence is an aid in coming to a conclusion: it supplies information within the conceptual framework of an investigation. It supplies a missing detail. When photographs are used in a control system, their evidence is more or less limited to establishing identity and presence. *But as soon as a photograph is used as a means of communication, the nature of lived experience is involved and then the truth becomes more complex.*

It is the third use of photography that raises more problematic issues since this kind of communication encompasses the notion of culture. It relies to a great extent on learnt and internalized attitudes, norms and ways of interpreting sociopolitical constructions. It is this cultural language and this '. . . range of unstated cultural assumptions that intrudes and indeed makes possible the communicative exchange of a photographer with an audience' (Webster, 1980, p. 18). The images that photographs create are drawn from and act upon already existing ideological and cultural assumptions.

Fortunately, '. . . agreement on the meaning of symbols is by no means shared by everyone in our culture . . . there are generally sub-cultures in existence whose particular ways of seeing influences the process of communication and creates a dissonance between communicator and audience' (ibid., p. 55).

However, according to the myth of the objective function of photography, someone would expect that photographed events or images would not include subjective emotions. In contrast, though, presented events are fully emotionally charged. Thus a picture alone is worth more than a thousand words. In even more complicated circumstances the emotions aroused by the photographed image are in contradiction to the written story accompanying the image. For instance, a charity organization may present a poster with two children with Down's syndrome followed by the caption 'THEY DO NOT NEED YOUR PITY, THEY NEED THEIR RIGHTS'. However, the way that the images are being presented may have been constructed in such a way as to arouse feelings of pity. In these circumstances the viewer receives two conflicting messages. The emotional message will overtake the written one, not only because emotions are stronger than words but also because the feeling of pity for 'the disabled' fits the prevalent dominant values.

In this case, the relation of photography and disability imagery raises other serious issues and needs an analysis itself. This was one among other issues that became the stimulus to expound my thinking about the social relation of photography and the creation of disability imagery.

DISABILITY IMAGES

Popular attitudes to disability have been highly influenced by the way disabled people are presented by visual means. As David Hewey (1992, p. 3) has argued: 'a photograph . . . which is based on a medical view (or model) of disability cannot lead to the empowerment and liberation of disabled people'. Most of the pictures of disabled people that surround us focus more on the impairment or disfigurement than the person. Consequently, when we have to make sense of such a picture our perception is dominated by the disfigurement and the feelings that it provokes in us. If we fear or reject the disfigurement then we fear or reject the person who has the disfigurement. The picture brings forward a physical sign that has been followed by socially and culturally constructed values that for years have left disabled people in oppressive and discriminatory situations.

The self and social images of disabled people have been determined by the images presented in pictures formed and used by non-disabled people. These images have been surrounded by the patronizing ideologies created by the same organizations that produced the visual appearances in the first place (i.e. charities). Dominant patronizing ideologies have associated disability with feelings of pity, fear and guilt, and with situations of dependence, cure and care. Hewey (1992, p. 24) offers us a critical in-depth analysis of why and how charity advertising has stabilized the low and oppressive status quo of disabled people. He argues that '. . . charity advertising serves as the calling-card of an inaccessible society which systematically segregates disabled people into both a social and physical reality by bonding the actual disablement of people with impairments, with the psychic fear in non-disabled people of the loss of ownership of their bodies'. Thus, the appearances of disabled people are being presented in such a way that a loss is being directly connected with disablement which in turn is connected with individual dysfunctionism. This is not a coincidence, bearing in mind the current political and economic directives that give priority to human functionality, consumerism, achievement, production and standards.

Moreover, photography and other visual means have strengthened the marginalization of disabled people, making them invisible by excluding them from other socially popular areas such as fashion in which the dominant image is that of the able-bodied. This exclusion is in accordance with the wider social practices of excluding them from the decision-making process that directly or indirectly affects their lives.

It is a matter of representation and equal opportunities for disabled people; the right of voice in the photographic production. In this context, disabled people have to struggle for alternative imagery that will empower them by presenting their spirit and their commitment to be part of their communities. It is a struggle against a notion of disability that negates and isolates the person and, at the same time, confirms and perpetuates segregated ideologies that exist in our culture. The alternative way of seeing and interpreting disability imagery is possible if disabled people are offered the opportunity to intervene and participate in the photography production and express their own perceptions about their self and social images.

To realize how disabled people have been presented and represented by the disability industry (including social agencies such as charities, mass media, special educational settings, medical organizations) we have to ask ourselves: Why do we perceive disabled people in the way we do? Why do we sometimes perceive them as dependent, socially dead, miserable, non-functional creatures that provoke feelings of pity, fear and guilt? Where do all these assumptions derive from? Is it only because they have one leg instead of two, or because they have low IQ (people with mental difficulties)? With whom do we compare them? And how do we construct this comparison? Why do we refer to the able-bodied as 'we' and to the disabled people as 'they'? How do we define this difference, where do we draw the line and from where have we been influenced to form our definitions and ways of seeing?

These questions seem to me to be very crucial as through my experiences I came to the realization that I do not act and think only as an individual in a vacuum but as part of a social-cultural system. The principles which informed the procedures of selecting a specific picture (while rejecting others) and the stories that the children of this study expressed in relation to the meaning they gave to the photograph strengthen my belief that, individually, we express societal priorities, needs, values and assumptions.

In the following discussion I am going to present some of the methodological dilemmas that emerged from the fieldwork. Most of the above ideas originated from these dilemmas that acted as stimuli for searching further about the role of visual communicative means.

USING PHOTOGRAPHS AS A METHODOLOGICAL TOOL IN ATTITUDINAL RESEARCH

The best way to start is by presenting two stories expressed by two children in their effort to give meaning to the picture they had in front of them:

> Lisa is 9 years old, she is tall with blonde long hair, she is beautiful, nice and clever. She is good at writing and reading, she is good at science and maths. She has lots of friends and today she went over to Sam's house to play with her. Sam is 8 years old, she cannot talk and walk properly. Her eyes are going inwards and her face is flabby. She is a bit disabled. She likes reading but she reads special books. They are both smiling because they are happy. They enjoy their friendship. Sometimes Lisa helps Sam to do things . . . Sam doesn't have lots of friends and she is naughty . . . I like Lisa to be my friend, she is cleverer . . . she looks brighter . . . I will invite Lisa to my party . . . [Why?] Because I like her hair, I don't know I just pick Lisa she is older.
>
> (Hellen, 8:2)

or

> Lisa and Sam are sisters. They have their arms around each other. They are sitting on the settee and they are talking. Lisa is 10 years old and Sam is 8. Lisa has lots of friends and sometimes she stands up for Sam because Sam is disabled and some people call her names . . . No Sam is not disabled, my mum is disabled. Sam is handicapped. My mum has problems with her legs but Sam has problems with her brain. She was born like that . . . Lisa is nice but sometimes she is tough because her eyes are like that and she is tall . . . She is clever because she is tall, she is blonde and beautiful . . . I like blondish . . . I will invite Sam to my party because she looks kind and she smiles and she helps people. If I pick Lisa then Sam won't have any friends.
>
> (Peter, 8:11)

and the stories go on. A hundred and three different children, a hundred and three different stories based on different or similar grounds, assumptions, values and cultural systems. 'We form impressions of other people when we meet them. We do this quite quickly and often on the basis of limited information. Which "bits" of information we use and which are the most important . . . and further to what extent our impressions of other people depend on our relationship to them?' (Thomas, 1978, p. 2). It is one thing to form impressions of the other in an actual encounter with him or her and another thing to create a whole biography about the other when he or she is a static image presented in a picture. That means that pictures in relation to the observer are given life. The use of a picture in attitudinal research has a double function. On one hand it enhances our understanding of how the 'visual image' of a static moment becomes dynamic and active when related to interpretations offered by the receiver. Even though '. . . we sometimes feel that the assertions a photograph makes – its statement – are so subtle and ineffable that they cannot be reduced to words' (Becker, 1979, p. 101), we do use this visual language of the picture as a stimulus in order to make our statements about the way we perceive what we see. Going further, '. . . we usually inspect . . . a photograph with an eye to answering some general questions about social arrangements or processes' (ibid., p. 104).

The creation of different general questions and the way we answer them is highly connected with our familial, social and cultural environment. This is exactly what a researcher wants to 'extract' from the participants when he or she introduces a picture in the methodological design of a study. He or she tries to explore and understand what kind of information the participants select from the available data – the picture – and the way(s) they interpret them. He or she endeavours to figure out the cues that, for different persons, become outstanding in the ways they make inferences. However, on the other hand, basing our assumptions and conclusions solely on the expressed opinions of the participants towards a snapshot can become quite misleading. Participants are called to express opinions and feelings about someone whom they have never encountered before in their everyday life. Whatever references they are going to make are based on some dominant cultural assumptions or on hypothetical suggestions. An example may illustrate what I mean by the above statement:

> An 8-year-old child expressed negative feelings towards the girl with Down's syndrome presented in the picture. She built a story in which she neglected the girl on the basis of her physical appearance. However, when we started discussing her interactions with some of her peers it was revealed that one of her best friends was a boy with Down's syndrome. Participant observation and familiarity with the children convinced me that the participant child was actually sharing activities with her peer with Down's syndrome. After discovering the same discrepancy, in other discussions, between children's opinions and feelings about the girl in the picture and their opinions and feelings about their actual peers with Down's syndrome, I became more sceptical about the way and the context in which I was going to use the picture.

First, the picture can be misleading if the children are asked only to offer their opinions and feelings towards the photographed girls. What is missing is vital: expression of opinions about the children's actual everyday interactions. As Firth and Rapley (1990) have suggested, repeated exposure to persons with disabilities changes people's expectations.

In the case where children expressed opinions only towards the two strangers in the picture the cue that became significant for the participants was the physique. 'A positively or negatively valued physique and appearance can mean the attribution of other personal qualities and characteristics which follow the value direction of the physical variation' (Thomas, 1978, p. 2). Thus it is at least unfair for both the participant and the individual in the picture to value and be valued respectively in an artificial/superficial way. Additionally this finding raises important issues about the selection of the picture that is going to be used as a methodological tool.

SELECTION OF THE PICTURE

It is inevitable that the way the person is being presented will somehow influence the response of the participant, at least in the initial phase of introducing the picture to him or her. The criteria used by the researcher in selecting the picture are significant when exploring the way the picture leads to responses.

One of the main ethical dilemmas I faced during the period when I was searching for the pictures for this study was the way that a person with Down's syndrome was going to be presented to the children. Down's syndrome is a visible disability and it encompasses not only disability stereotypes but also exploits cultural stereotypes of physical beauty. Additionally there were two technical problems that impeded the finding of the 'adequate' picture. Most of the pictures I had found presented physically disabled people. There were very few pictures presenting children with Down's syndrome and these pictures portrayed the child in an isolated way. Things became more complicated as I had to take into consideration issues such as the age and gender of the persons in the picture and of the participant children. Retrospectively it seems to me that every bit of the picture, even things that had escaped my observation, were significant in children's eyes, who proved to be better observers than I was.

After the pilot process with three pictures I found that, if I was to be able to keep the conversation in focus, especially with very young children, the picture should not present more than two persons. Otherwise, fascinated by what they see, children may create imaginative stories involving not the target persons of the picture but the persons that they want to involve in their stories. These stories can enhance our understanding of the children's world but may be irrelevant to the purpose of the study.

For these reasons the picture which proved to fulfil the demands of the study included two female individuals, sitting together, smiling and having their arms around each other.

Cook (1971) and Argyle (1975) argue that the process of forming impressions of others is a complicated affair involving static elements – the face in response, physique, clothes, hairstyles, cosmetics, etc. – and dynamic aspects such as orientation, distance, posture, gesture, body movement, facial expression, gaze and directions (in Thomas, 1978, p. 6). The picture selected for the study included both static and dynamic elements and this inclusion was one of the reasons for presenting two individuals together. The facial expressions, the distance between the two girls, the gaze, were carefully selected so as to project a 'dynamic interaction' in a static snapshot. The images presented brought forward a positively orientated moment. Thus the picture was not introduced to present or to emphasize an 'impairment' but an interaction between a disabled and a non-disabled person.

Moreover, the picture was contextualized as it was presented to specific groups of children. These children were experiencing an academic environment in which they were being educated with children with Down's syndrome. Certainly, the picture would have had a different impact in a different environment. These are parameters that should be taken into consideration before the researcher selects the picture, and when he or she tries to make sense of the children's responses.

Some responses may mislead the researcher as he or she is not aware of what were the 'symbols' of the picture that became the stimulus and with what experiences they were linked in the child's mind, influencing his or her responses. Often static elements of the picture hide social values and in children's perception are linked with functional effectiveness, intellectuality and likeability. Thus the researcher should probe for further explanations.

For instance, one of the two girls in the picture (Lisa, the non-disabled girl) was characterized by some children as 'clever', 'brighter' and 'older' than Sam (the girl with Down's syndrome). In some cases after probing it was revealed that children based their assumptions and expectations on a symbol, the watch, that indicates knowledge of time – an abstract and quite complicated concept to be comprehended by children. The fact that Lisa was wearing a watch meant that she knew the time; thus she was cleverer than Sam who didn't wear a watch. The age of the children was important in relation to the way they interpreted the same symbol: for younger children a watch indicated knowledge, for older children, especially females, it indicated elegance.

If further probing had not taken place I would have remained with the idea that it was the disability signs which provoked such responses, whereas it was another symbol that transmitted social messages as well. There are many such cues in a picture which follow the value direction of the external appearance. Statements such as 'Lisa is bright because she is tall, blonde and beautiful' or 'Sam is kind because of her eyes' are not value free. Such cues project unique sociopsychological functions that should be taken into consideration both prior to the selection of the picture and during the discussions about the context of the picture.

Finally, there were two further principles which informed the selection process: a research-based and an ethical-based principle. 'Since pictures often contain a wealth of information it is not surprising that more than one true thing can be said on the basis of a single image. When this happens, it only means that we are asking different questions which deserve and get different answers' (Becker, 1979, p. 106).

Thus the picture was introduced in order to provide the opportunity to the students to ask their own questions and offer their own answers instead of only the researcher asking predetermined questions. Moreover, as they were responding to the picture they were simultaneously revealing some of the sources from which they had obtained the information they were offering. I suspect that the combination of using a picture in group discussions offered breadth and depth to the responses of the children. My experience shared something of what Ann Lewis (1992, p. 415) experienced when having group interviews with children:

> They were prompting one another with reference to things not known to the interviewer and this enabled individual children to amplify their responses . . . their effectiveness may reflect the absence of the sorts of features (such as highly specific questions, and questions rather than comments) which diminish the quality and quantity of children's talk in conversation with adults.

A further rationale for using the picture was based on the assumption, which was qualified throughout the process, that initial encounters with disabled people do not start from a neutral point. As Thomas (1978, p. 8) claimed: '. . . the disabled person has to deal with definitions of himself and his disability previously and independently conceived by others.' The introduction of the picture offered the opportunity for an artificial initial encounter between the participant children and the disabled girl of the picture, and in turn children's predefinitions and preconceptions about a disabled person were revealed.

In addition, however, to exploring children's predefinitions, I was interested in their perceptions about their everyday lived experiences/interactions with peers who had Down's syndrome. By asking children to reveal their perceptions about their peers with Down's syndrome unavoidably I had to differentiate the six children with Down's syndrome being educated at this school. Such a differentiation encompasses the danger of categorizing and labelling children not previously labelled by their peers in their social educational environment.

Therefore, the effect of such discussions about particular children may have a negative influence on their social integration. The group discussions had to take such a form as to control the possibility of no one becoming 'a subject under scrutiny'. The picture was used as a means to achieve this aim as it smoothed out the transition from hypothetical-fictional interactions to more concrete daily based social encounters. This combination – hypothetical/ fictional and concrete daily based interactions – became retrospectively the source of the following issue that a researcher should take into consideration.

AN ISSUE FOR CONSIDERATION

Reflecting on the group discussions with the children, it became evident that a picture of a disabled person brings out a more negative perspective if compared to the perspective they had about their peers with Down's syndrome. This is likely to be related to the fact that the children came in contact with the people of the picture only once. The first was the last time as well. In their reality they had the chance to come in contact with their disabled peers on a daily basis. Thus even though initially it was the appearance which influenced their reaction towards them, afterwards there were other characteristics which became more significant (i.e. personality, shared activities, mutuality, testing or stereotypes and prejudices, demystification of myths through lived experiences).

What was missing from the encounter with the individuals in the picture was a second or even multiple chance for '. . . an active search for confirmatory evidence' (Hargreaves, 1982, p. 33). Perceiving people and making inferences about them is a continuous process in which many changes take place from our initial assumptions. If that is the case, then what we have from the participant receiver of the picture is his or her initial reactions and assumptions about the other. Thus we cannot talk about a process but rather about a static initial encounter. As Hargreaves (ibid.) stresses regarding the way we perceive the other: '. . . people are prepared to make inferences on the basis of the most slender evidence that so many of our initial inferences about other people are misleading and sometimes completely false.' Triangulation of the responses is one way to offer an opportunity for the participants to express the various 'selves' they present in different situations; it is also valuable for increasing the researcher's opportunities for understanding and approaching the participant's perceptions, opinions, feelings and actions towards the other to the degree that this is possible.

CONCLUSION

The aim of this chapter was not to reach any final conclusions but to begin a discussion regarding the relationship between methods and the creation as well as the interpretation of realities. Even though the main focus was on the use of photography as a methodological tool it was shown that the methods we use are neither neutral nor objective. The decision to use a photograph was based on the assumption that its mechanisms construct images and identities which often can be misleading.

Additionally, it was based on the assumption that the use of photography is an enabling mechanism for revealing social and cultural norms which in turn can be under analysis and demystification. These assumptions were qualified throughout the process of using the photograph within a research context. However, in doing so it was necessary to reflect critically on the social history of the method, and its use in particular contexts.

Further, our ideological view – according to which interactions with disabled people do not start from a neutral point and do not originate solely from the characteristics that the disabled individual poses – played its own role in selecting this method. Using a photograph was perceived as a suitable method for investigating social interactions among non-disabled and disabled children because it offered the opportunity to explore the 'starting-point' from which children's perceived initial encounters with disabled children.

Finally, a strong realization throughout the research process was that the selection of different methods is related to the way we define aspects of the paramount reality (Cohen and Taylor, 1976) within which both the researcher and the participants act. In order to understand the created definitions of this reality it is deemed necessary to share the way of acting and thinking that leads us to view reality from a certain ideological/methodological perspective. I do not feel that admitting the effects and the constraints we pose in defining the field sacrifices objectivity; rather, and in response to fears that by doing so the objective dimension of research is at stake, I think that no research can become objective unless we share, reflect upon and evaluate the perspective from which we approach different aspects of reality.

REFERENCES

Aloia, G. and MacMillan, D. (1983) 'Influence of the EMR label on initial expectations of regular-classroom teachers', *American Journal of Mental Deficiency*, Vol. 88, no. 3, pp. 255–62.

Bak, J. and Siperstein, G. (1986) 'Protective effects of the label "mentally retarded" on children's attitudes toward mentally retarded peers', *American Journal of Mental Deficiency*, Vol. 91, no. 1, pp. 95–7.

Becker, H. (1979) 'Do photographs tell the truth?', in T. Cook and C. Reichardt (eds) *Qualitative and Quantitative Methods in Evaluation Research*. Sage, London.

Berger, J. and Mohr, J. (1982) *Another Way of Telling*. Writers & Readers Publishing, London.

Besag, V. (1989) *Bullies and Victims in Schools*. Open University Press, Milton Keynes.

Bogdan, R. and Knopp, S. (1982) *Qualitative Research for Education: An Introduction to Theory and Methods*. Allyn & Bacon, Boston, Mass.

Cohen, S. and Taylor, L. (1976) *Escape Attempts: The Theory and Practice of Resistance to Everyday Life*. Pelican Books, Harmondsworth.

Delamont, S. and Hamilton D. (1993) 'Revisiting classroom research: a continuing cautionary tale', in Hammersley, M. (ed.) *Controversies in Classroom Research*, Milton Keynes, Open Unversity Press.

English, D. E. (1981) *Political Uses of Photography in the Third French Republic 1871–1914*. UMI Research Press, Ann Arbor, Michigan.

Firth, H. and Rapley, M. (1990) *From Acquaintance to Friendship: Issues for People with Learning Disabilities*. BIMH Publications, Birmingham.

Freire, P. (1985) *The Politics of Education: Culture, Power and Liberation*. Macmillan, London.

Goffman, E. (1976) *Stigma: Notes on the Management of Spoiled Identity*. Pelican Books, Harmondsworth.

Gottlieb, J. (1974) 'Attitudes towards retarded children: effects of labeling and academic performance', *American Journal of Mental Deficiency*, Vol. 79, no. 3, pp. 268–73.

Hargreaves, D. (1982) *The Challenge for the Comprehensive School*. Routledge & Kegan Paul, London.

Hewey, D. (1992) *The Creatures Time Forgot: Photography and Disability Imagery*. Routledge, London.

Kennedy, A. and Hurman, K. (1982) 'Inclinations of nonhandicapped children to help their handicapped peers', *The Journal of Special Education*, Vol. 16, no. 3, pp. 319–27.

Lewis, A. (1992) 'Group child interviews as a research tool', *British Educational Research Journal*, Vol. 18, no. 4, pp. 413–21.

Siperstein, G., Bak, J. and O'Keefe, P. (1988) 'Relationship between children's attitudes toward and their social acceptance of mentally retarded peers', *American Journal of Mental Deficiency*, Vol. 93, no. 1, pp. 24–7.

Siperstein, G., Gottlieb, J. and Bak, J. (1976) 'Effects of group discussion on children's attitudes toward handicapped peers', *Journal of Educational Research*, Vol. 11, pp. 131–4.

Thomas, D. (1978) *The Social Psychology of Childhood Disability*. Cambridge University Press.

Thomas, D. (1982) *The Experience of Handicap*. The Chaucer Press, London.

Walker, R. and Wiedel, J. (1985) 'Using photographs in a discipline of words', in R. Burgess (ed.) *Field Methods in the Study of Education*. Falmer Press, Lewes.

Webster, F. (1980) *The New Photography: Responsibility in Visual Communication*. Whitstable Litho, Kent.

9

PROBLEMS OF IDENTITY AND METHOD IN THE INVESTIGATION OF SPECIAL EDUCATIONAL NEEDS

Peter Clough

> It is not your system or clear sight that mills
> Down small to the consequence a life requires.
>
> (William Empson)

An organizing concept of this chapter is that of identity: my own identity as a researcher and the identities of the teachers whose lives occupy the ground of the research. The ways in which these identities are mutually constructive raises questions about the nature of special educational needs, and about the research methods which presume to address them. The scene of the chapter is a study, funded by ESRC, called 'Constructions of Special Educational Need'.[1]

The chapter reflects a concern of mine at the moment about educational research generally. The experience of carrying out – and, more, of trying to report – quite a large funded study led me to a number of questions about the fitness of methods as we know and use them in educational research to offer insight into human experience.

The chapter wonders – and wanders – about this as a loose thesis:

> Method in social science subverts a profound human impulse to tell stories about the world as we see it. Method undoes the truth, for we put in method a trust it could not start to understand, being without feeling. We ask method to do something – to validate our work – which we cannot do ourselves. All method can do – or at least method as we know it in the social sciences – all method can do is reflect back to us our lack of engagement with our work, a lack we must announce as the very condition of our professionalism.

ORIGINS OF THE RESEARCH

Special educational needs are understood here as something constructed by people in ways which are continuous with the structure of their lives; as having an identity, that is, which makes particular sense to those people in terms provided by the experience of their lives. But we also understand that people themselves work within contexts which have themselves a sediment of particular meaning as a function of their identity; that to work in a given post in a particular school or office is to take a place within a system of given meanings. So the task for the individual is not a wholly uphill one; he or she enters a field of meanings already to hand and – to greater or lesser extent – indispensably takes on the shared task of realizing institutional meanings.

Now what was interesting for me, what prompted the study, was how the identity of the individual meets with the identity of the institution, and in turn that of the larger community; how, that is, the one so acts on the other as to change it. This is happening dynamically all the time, in every action and interaction. In a sense, the very (UK) legislation (of 1981, that is) insists on such a view for in approximating SEN as situationally relative the central policy makes a problematic of policy itself; policy is to some extent to be determined according to local priorities, local identities.

In the proposal for funding by the ESRC I wrote:

> The issues and practices of integration make many, often threatening demands on teachers, who may be required to develop new roles and new ways of working within new and unpredictable systems . . . Such changes in policy clearly depend for their success to an important degree on the professional orientation and motivation of the staffs who are charged with realizing them. If teachers are seen as mediators of policy at classroom and school levels in this way, then – both for the evaluation of that policy and for its development – we need to be able to identify and describe the ways in which teachers engage with and feel about their work. In the field of special needs, we need to know more about the fundamental conceptions of practice with which special needs teachers operate: to what extent are they continuous with those of mainstream practitioners? Are there dimensions of difference reflecting differing views of learning, and of learning difficulty? How are the two cultures (of Special and mainstream practice) related in the practice of classroom teachers?

This idea had been coming a long time. I had first noticed it in Croll and Moses' *One in Five* (1985), where they talk about primary schoolteachers' preferences for different sorts of information about children with difficulties. I had worked *as* an educational psychologist years ago, and saw often in teachers that barely contained need to know what was a child's IQ; not what he or she can do nor where he or she had been in school before but: What's the raw material we're working with here? This tendency to a ready causality issues in so many casual staffroom attributions: well he's not very bright; well, she comes from a notorious family; her brother was . . . The drive, so often, is towards reaching to the shelf for so many ready-made, sedimented and superficial 'explanations' subtended in every use – though surely mostly unconsciously – by a wealth of ideological, historical and indeed many other values.

And I wondered simply where these ideas – about what is 'wrong' with children – came from in the lives of these teachers. I've since much changed my mind about the way ideas arrive in people's lives and so infect their thinking; but in the early days of thinking fitfully about this idea I supposed that you could open up people's heads, as it were, by talking to them almost without end about their lives; their fears and excitements and failures and passions; their children, their parents, their lovers even. More formally, they might be asked to say quite simply 'how they see it', what beliefs and principles inform their thought and, more, their action. In a way you could say I had an idea that I could discover a crucial piece of programming; as it were, the chip that organized the network of professional behaviour. This is of course a gross metaphor.

And I had stored a suggestion made by John Wilson and Barbara Cowell (1984) who wrote in a paper called 'How shall we define handicap?':

> We have to find out what principles and assumptions control the thinking (and hence the decisions) of those concerned [with SEN]; and that means interacting with and conversing with them, not merely issuing them with questionnaires or seeing what they have to say in structured interviews. For . . . the assumptions are often hidden; not only from the interviewer but from the person interviewed. Much time and effort is required to grasp the shape and style of a person's deepest thoughts.

Their observations gave me the seed of a method, too, as they went on (ibid.):

> In the case of handicap and 'special' children, it would be unwise to start from any particular view about identification and treatment; we need rather . . . to map out the views and concepts of people in the business without any implication that they measure up, or fail to measure up to a pre-established picture.

And another burr that had stuck to me: speaking of the relationship between the individual and society, Raymond Williams (1965) says: 'These real issues can only be looked at adequately if we recognize the continuity between the many kinds of organization which compose the whole living process. To abstract certain fixed states and then argue from them, which has been the normal method of approaching this question is wholly inadequate.' Williams became very important to me; bear with this extensive quotation: in '. . . exploring the fundamental relation between organism and organisation' he says of the genesis of that relation (ibid.):

In interpreting and describing our experience we develop a particular system in terms of which we then live. Every organism both embodies and continues an organization of this kind. Its purpose is the reception and communication of experience in such a form that by adjustment and action the organization itself, and therefore the particular life of the organism, can be continued. Each one of us has within an apparently separate individuality a system of observing, selecting, comparing, adjusting and acting as elaborate and complex as any social system yet described.

The organism, then, generates organization; but this individual organization is crucially related to organizations 'outside' itself, a much larger organization with which it is in certain radical ways continuous. So the point of Williams' exploration can be redefined (ibid.): 'We are seeking to define and consider one central principle: that of the essential relation, the true interaction, between patterns learned and created in the mind and patterns communicated and made active in relationships, conventions and institutions.' The generic term which Williams uses for the process of these patterns and relationships is culture. Culture describes the embodiment of institutions in individuals, the investment of individuals in institutions. Using Williams' terms we can begin to understand the ways in which the conception and organization of SEN provision and inquiry can be seen as a particular and distinct culture; how this culture has evolved a powerful 'language of the tribe' which reinforces its distinctness and minimizes its accessibility to other communities; and, perhaps most importantly, how research in the field is determined by the same culture, but fails to recognize its cultural nature and organization and cannot, hence, easily initiate or mediate reform. Most SEN research maintains this culture unself-consciously – that is to say, critically unaware of itself – because it has no properly ontological intent; while it continues to take for granted the objects which, actually, it produces it cannot but effectively celebrate the realization of forms of difference (although it may rail against their moral and political effects).

'Yet sometimes we suppose,' says Williams (ibid.),

> that we can state the substances of individual, society and material world in such a way that there are no relationships between them until, as it were, some signal is given, and having defined the substances as in themselves they are, we can go on now to study the relations between them. But in fact these substances are forms of relationship which we can never finally isolate, since the organization throughout is in interlocking terms. We begin to realize, from experience, that the relationships are inherent, and that each organization is, precisely, an embodiment of relationships, the lived and living history of responses to and from other organizations. Organization, that is to say, is enacted in the organism,

and here it is finally: '*to know either fully is to know the other*' (ibid.), (emphasis added).

There were others – like the similar echo of structure in Wright Mills's relation of 'private troubles and public issues' – but in Croll and Moses, in Wilson and Cowell and in Williams I had a context and the glimpse, if not the tools, of a method all coherent in a way of viewing life.

LIVING POLICY

Practice is a tightly woven fabric; pull on one thread only and the whole puckers: see the teacher clearly and the structures which find him or her in their places are discovered. So open up the place of work that he or she is revealed within it. This is surely the ethnographic task *par excellence.*

Organism and organization, this was the point: to see what common aspects of structure and which of culture bound teachers and the contexts in which they worked; how, that is to say, policies worked through individuals, often silently and without their knowing; but, more so even, how policies are made by teachers. The point is an important one if we are to understand how the present system of SEN provision is supported not merely in the structures of society (such as its institutions) but necessarily – on pain of ceasing to exist – in the structures of experience of the individuals who participate in that culture.

For against our experience and sometimes our judgement, we live, I live, with a naïve, a thoroughly top-down, hierarchical notion of policy. Policy is 'made' up there somewhere – in Whitehall, in Washington or Victoria – and filters through local offices: local education authorities, regional bodies who each pull on it in its passage to (something known oppositionally as) practice. Schools, again, arrest it, and make it this or they make it that; departments or faculties lay a hand on it until it is still in the classroom (and in the corridor, the playground and the dining-room). And all this while – in this account – the teacher *apparently* awaits the signal that will license his or her action (see, for example, Fulcher, 1989).

Or, start the other way and in laying bare what teachers do you will not explain or even describe their actions without recourse – going the other way – to the trace of decisions which serially mediate ideology with resources.

This sort of polarization reflects a 'natural attitude' deep in the culture which says this is how it works. The record of empirical research in the area bears it out. In the main, studies of special needs practice have been concentrated within specific levels of organization – for example, the LEA or the school – rather than describing the structural intervolvement of different sites of experience, from the individual through departments, schools, LEAs to the national context and beyond.

At the end of the notional line, though, not much has been done with what individual teachers do and think about what they do (nor, significantly, on *what* what they do does). To be sure, teacher attitudes (to integration, for example) have been investigated, though largely independently of context; such studies typically ask teachers to respond in terms of stereotypes, or of hypothetical situations (though among few exceptions, Bines, 1986, for example, located investigation of teacher professional orientations in the context of school organization).

Three points emerge from this sketch. First, of course, all such studies may (though often implicitly) refer across levels of context, but they most frequently do so for the initial purposes of identifying a sample, and subsequent discussion coheres largely around the specific organizational level of that targeted sample. Secondly, studies of teachers' experience and thinking in this area have been rudimentary and have not been related to larger policy context; studies have not required teachers critically to relate their views and practice to the experienced effects of policy. But mostly, such studies show no sensitivity to the complexity of jointly implicated personal and professional life events; what is required at this level is a much richer exploration of the seam of subjective experience than is indicated in the study of mere attitudes.

But we have come to see teachers as sorts of indifferently 'black boxes' whose actions can be explained in terms of policies, and there is at work here an assumption that we can explain what teachers do in terms of the policy contexts in which they work; that somehow what they do will be more simply but no less causally understood if we know the policies which appear to give those actions a coherence.

Well, to be sure we cannot understand what teachers do without knowing something of these contexts. But what people like Peter Woods, for example, have been at pains to try to show is how behaviours – for want of a better word; and it is mine, not his – inevitably reveal patterns created in the mind in another time (and in other policy contexts). Life-historical study is thus driven by a sort of search for fossils – in the texts constructed in interview – which give a sense and an index of those other times; it is the researcher's task then to trace how those other times lead in the instance of this or that subject to the very present constitution of a self, and of the set of practices which define it.

For it must – it must – be true that what teachers do in classrooms is policy; not, that is to say, *makes* or even realizes policy: *is* policy. After the words in committee and the documents in the filing-cabinets, how ever else should we come to know the life of policy other than in classroom life? This is to go beyond Macdonald's (1981) typology of policy as written, stated and/or enacted, and to see the meaning of policy as revealed in the surplus of experience over structure; it is what what we do does – and feels like – when the texts, the statements and the observations have been counted.

But this calls for a method which – though sensitive as possible; sensitive as sensitive can be, even – is still a method and, as such, demands disengagement on the part of the researcher.

NICK, PAUL AND ME

In one of the Midlands schools we studied, we spent something like 300 days over two years mainly talking to staff within the scope and schedule of the project. Now this school was of great interest: a big (about 2,000 students) place fairly downtown in a big city tired with industrial collapse; fitfully tense – in this retrenchment – with a substantial Pakistani community brought so many years ago thousands of miles indifferently as so many operatives; and made slightly famous by local politicians who polarized each other into caricatures of left and right (one Labour councillor described the Tory leader – in his presence – as ''itler wi' knobs on'; this without a smile).

Of a staff of over 140, some eight were employed full time as special educators, mainly supporting children in mainstream classrooms; a further eight worked as language support teachers with the many students whose first tongue was not English. This is by any standard a high proportion of teachers in support-for-access roles.

I shall tell the whole story elsewhere, but in brief there were many mutterings about these support departments, and in particular about the special needs organization; it was falling apart and was become friable as its head of department. My hunch was that when Nick, the head of department, was vigorous, the whole show thrived, was large with his presence and verve. He was, he is, actually large. He moved heavily and always sought his breath. He smoked heavily. He is Irish and it is true that he all but sings his words.

Few structures held the department together beyond those which organized his own spirit. To be sure, there were timetables, a policy of sorts, schedules for staff to refer children for help. But I insist that these were contingent, mere stuff that routed Nick's energy.

So it was simple: when Nick began to fall apart – as his dying wife suffered on and on – the department, too, sagged. Thus, phenomenally, lessons were missed, reports unfiled, departmental meetings cancelled, case conferences ill-prepared . . . But, really, these were only things to point to later in the account when the infection of the department needed a name. What really happened was a matter in the nerves.

And Nick sat the while holding a court among the dozen or so smokers who had been granted a separate common-room. A 15-minute break mid-morning is just long enough for two cigarettes end-on if you leave your lesson sharp enough on the bell and will be always a moment or two late for the class at 11. If you really have to see Nick you must find him in this smoky room.

I spent probably 30 hours with Nick, about 15 of them on tape. I learnt his personal history and the record of his professional work. I learnt, I think – as Wilson and Cowell have it – the shape of his thought, his innermost feelings.

And, for the record, you could say that here was a life that could only be lived as indeed it had, and to the point it had: the fossils of class, family, schooling (coloured in turn by poverty, warmth and failure) were there to see if see them you would.

And I became so occupied with Nick that his presence simply organized my whole sense of the school and, indeed, of the project.

I did not realize that I had shed a conventional researcher identity until some time later when, indeed, the funded part of it was over, and what remained was the writing-up. I had some study leave, and I arranged to spend the first two weeks – immediately following the New Year, in a holiday flat on the Yorkshire coast. The town was cold, deserted and my flat looked simply over the dull North Sea.

I had brought the data, mainly transcribed interviews, but for two days I wrote nothing. I had thought to do something with Nick, with Nick's data. I read again and again the transcriptions; highlighted parts. What I wanted to do was to write a life history that would show his life in special education; show the life of special education in him.

I had had, some 12 months before, a previous go at this sort of job and had appalled myself at the outcome. I had taken the life – or the documents of the life – of a man in the study, Paul; a man whose identity with his era and generation seemed to me, at the time, so distinct that his words as they came from the transcript made up badges of rank or time served, or of skills rewarded and campaigns followed.

I had been excited by the scent of a 'case'; I saw the story – or, rather, the issues – which made this life coherent for me. It was a model life: overcoming a drunken father and a pathological family, a steelworker (born in 1922) so improves himself by his own efforts that he rises to become a clerk with some responsibility; he marries and has three sons. He remains a socialist and a slightly sceptical methodist (and certainly a teetotaller) for most of his life. Two of the boys go to grammar school, and then to university. They are four and six years older than Paul, my subject, and they bring home with them communism and poetry. Paul goes to a secondary modern school where he is moved by the 'dedication' of an English teacher. And he is increasingly aware of children about him who are unfortunate in this way or that. He goes on a CND march; he cries in Deane Park the day the Wilson government falls. He goes to a teacher training college in London where, during a teacher practice in Tower Hamlets, he is drawn to another strong man who teaches 'the remedials' (and Paul knows 'there and then' his vocation). He is now head of special education in a large inner-city comprehensive school and lives distinctly in its catchment; he is branch secretary of the Labour Party; he has a season ticket on the Kop and runs a (girls') soccer team; he teaches Sunday school; he . . .

More? It goes on as I make it go on. I don't know how much of it is 'true' (and checking the transcriptions will throw little light on that). But when I tried to bring Paul off the page, all that would come was the print of so many clearly paid-up memberships; the print of the badges.

After three days of looking for Nick in these other transcriptions, I found him in my imagination. He had spoken to me of his wife, I knew something of her illness and the demands it made of Nick's life. And I remembered a morning quite early in my relationship with Nick when he took his cigarette to his mouth then pushed his hand quickly away and said *Christ I stink of shit*. I laughed and he said *I was up half the night, Jen's incontinent now*.

But what I wrote was made in my own store of knowledge and, free of the facts, seemed to say more of Nick and Nick in school than ever he had said or could have said. For all sorts of reasons this is not the place to reproduce that writing (and I am indeed still struggling to find the voice which will affront neither Nick nor the reader, but will at the same time do justice to the act of imagination which illuminated my understanding of the continuities of Nick's life). I simply had a vision of Nick looking after his wife in the night, a vision organized by the pathos of my own life.

This became for me the moment of realization of the ultimately positivist drive of my project to understand others; for in excitedly attaching the organism/organization idea – and eagerly attaching badges to analyse that relationship – I had forgotten my own insertion in this particular culture: the organism that was/is me and which would inevitably mediate whatever I saw and felt. And my 'understanding of others' – in this case Nick and his school – came not from the data spilling from the tea chests, nor from any reading of the literature but, indeed, from a setting aside of those things; and from a simple act of imagination that could only have sprung from my own experience. It doesn't matter whether what I wrote about Nick in the night took place in fact; it takes place in an act of imagination driven by profound symbols; the event symbolizes in a way which data and analysis could never do.

But the story of Nick, though unique in its particularity, is not actually a dramatic, outstanding 'case'. There were many others which I began to see (or, rather, to give this form to) in the project. Let me briefly tell one other here.

In another school, an almost bizarre structure somehow permitted within the same special needs department two wholly, but wholly, independent systems of in-class support, on the one hand, and withdrawal on the other. But as far as I could see the only *real* principle of organization of this division was sexual orientation; the head of department was so profoundly unnerved by the fact that her deputy was a lesbian that, quite simply, she could not even speak to her, and thus two subdepartments ostensibly driven by deep ideological differences coexisted silently.

In each of these – and in many other such – cases, the stories come from information '. . . that normal science recommends we discount, control or ignore' (as Pym, 1990 observes of his own similar attempts): 'Facts in this situation start as events which fail to elaborate a framework.' And this urge to find their story come from what Inglis (1993, p. 153) calls '. . . the foundation faculty of the human mind which is its propensity for story-telling'. What I am trying to get at here has an application beyond research in special education (though it has a peculiarity which I shall talk of later).

BODIES OF RESEARCH

There are, for argument's sake, two contrary directions in educational research at this time, and they involve movements in polarized direction.[2] The one, for argument's sake, largely takes its terms and instruments for granted, and all that remains is to gather data to feed those designs which are given with the instruments (for example, many large-funded programmes); this is a process, then, of *addition,* and it is an endless process. The other, for argument's sake, is that more recent occupation of educational research with the researcher him- or herself and their very insertion in the process of research (e.g. teacher/and some action research programmes); this activity endlessly problematizes terms and instruments, and so is a process of subtraction; of talking away, that is, the methodologically impure, the ideologically suspect.[2]

This antimony of outward and inward seems of much more use – because of greater moral importance – than the traditional (and merely contingent) ones of qualitative/quantitative, empiricist/rationalist and so on – though they may be logically cognate. But cognition is a trick here; it matters more that these traditional polarizations are not *morally necessitated.* They are functions of method which does not, of itself, carry any moral charge; and it is surely the drive to some revelation of the author's moral engagement with his or her topic that lies (or should lie) behind this inward-seeking trend of self-conscious research.

Reflections on research collected, for example, by Burgess (1985), Walford (1991) and Vulliamy and Webb (1992) emphasize the growing critical but also reflective self-awareness of educational inquiry, and in the introductions to each of these collections you can see the impulse to such revelation located and justified in a particular tradition of human science study. In respect of the latter, Walford's reminder that most such self-conscious inquiry is undertaken by qualitatively orientated researchers reminds us that may be, but only may be, quantitative procedures may not be susceptible to this sort of treatment. If this is so, then it is not because such researchers are not brought morally to their work, but that those forms of inquiry appear to depend for their validity on an elevation of method over personal engagement.

Of course, one of the effects of what might be called research councilism is that the majority of studies have lost any connectedness with epistemology and ontology; this is to say that they proceed along well-sedimented channels which take their objects and the instruments which investigate them for granted; there may be curiosity but seldom if ever any radical astonishment, any concern really to problematize phenomena in terms of their moral and political colour.

Contextualization of the study in hand is confined to limited and endlessly inter- and intrareferring literature which shores up its own claims. And it is customary to show how clean were the instruments used by arguing their distinctness from us as persons; look, we would typically say, they have been used by Smith, and Jones and Brown (1954, 1988 and 1977); and as they are not of them so they are not of us. All the drive of this 'methodology' is towards saying: there is no infection here. But this emphasis on instrumentation means also that what is ultimately missing from the study is any real engagement of values – for instruments themselves don't have values.

It is not incidental that the research report is, in the main, a text characterized by an austerity of language which makes it hard to read (and this is probably a fair example of that!); it is in the nature of research to suppress the so-called subjective responses of the researcher, or at least to force these within the frame of an indifferent scheme. The researcher puts instruments between herself and her object. She has to, because the researcher must show that her understanding always refers to a scheme of things constituted by the community. It can hardly be surprising, then, that in the research report the communicative functions of language are elevated over its expressive qualities. The language of research must serve to render the object not as the researcher sees it in experience, but as a research community would have it, as so many data whose validity can be checked and referenced. These checks, these references maintain the language of the tribe.

Some case studies, some ethnographies give the lie to this view. But if you look at how they do this – how the ones which really 'work' for you do this – then surely it is because they strain at their own given form; they seek to push back the restraints of given form, to form anew, to innovate form on pain of failing to express what the writer feels must be expressed. And, where these studies work, there is surely some surplus of meaning over the cold, lexical qualities which language usually demonstrates in the research report.

What is it, ultimately, that is persuasive about this or that piece of research? It is surely not – at the level of meaning – its claim to 'validity'. We are not led in the first instance to affirm a view, given with a research report, by some elegance of validation, but by its manifest (and manifestly taken-for-granted) ability to speak to our experience because it shares our objects. We use a hidden aesthetic really to evaluate any account; does this account, Bolton (1981) asks (echoing Hume), '. . . contain any metaphor which reveals a reality deeper than common sense? No? Does it excite you to a moral involvement in the affairs with which it deals? No? Commit it then to the flames, for it is nothing but information that will soon be superseded by more information'. The process at work always is one not of validation, but of verification. Of course, the 'research attitude' is right when it speaks of demanding validation in terms of the object and not of the inquirer. But the real meaning of its drive to 'objectivity' is revealed when, in its provision of the validation it requires, it fails to distinguish between the object proper and the characterizations which instruments themselves produce.

Think of the start of a research process: there is a researcher and there is a situation of objects which he or she must constitute. At this point there occurs a critical moment of characterization, which determines those objects for the researcher and audience. This is the moment normally referred to as methodological, and which as such is the correlate of the later process of validation; indeed, it is all that validation can reveal: is the method what it set out to be, what its author says it is? For validation is based on a limited model of truth which either takes for granted, or else ignores, the earlier process of verification which guarantees its coherence.

For verification stands in relation to validation as does understanding to explanation: in each case they precede. Validation is a gloss on verification, and attention to validation is in effect an attention to method at the expense of attending to the object which the method should reveal.

RESEARCH IN SEN

There have been many calls over the last 15 or so years for an empirical research in special education which would treat more sensitively of the matter and experience of learning difficulties. Schindele (1985) cites as a major priority in respect of research objectives the exploration of meanings, of subjective definitions and complex relationships; citing Wolf and Tymitz (1976) he says that research must '. . . aim at understanding actualities, social realities and human perceptions'; of primary importance is the '. . . understanding [of] human behaviour from the subject's own frame of reference' (Bogdan and Biklen, 1982). It should be emphasized that Schindele is making these comments in the context of a wide-ranging overview of the field of special education research; a particular significance of these observations is the limited space which they occupy in a review which is otherwise largely taken up with typifications of the quantitative methodologies which have dominated the field.

To be sure, Schindele (1985) calls for 'more adequate and more systematic application of qualitative research methodology'; and this is taken up later in the same collection of papers by Corrie and Zaklukievicz (1985) whose quotation from Eggleston (1974) is instructive: '. . . the "scientific" conception of the everyday world that has to be adopted in order to act in a scientific way is at variance with the subtle, shifting and often covert everyday conceptions of the world and the responses to it that are at the heart of what is being studied', and '. . . the dissonance between methodology and phenomena in education has in consequence become more manifest, the central issue here being the capacity of purely quantitative procedures to generate an adequate understanding of the reality of educational institutions'. But – and the point needs to be made again and again – can this ever be a field which could rid itself of an essentially quantitative character, conditioned as it is in the medico-psychological tradition? Can research hope to break out of this? What methods would be up to achieving this? And to method, what value should attach?

We are a long way from realizing that research in the social sciences will only find in its theatres of inquiry what it puts there. And this is particularly true of the field of SEN, whose origins in the measurement of behaviour endure as stark functions of policy.

For special education is pre-eminently a world of paid-up meanings and attributions; in experience it issues from and is set about with meanings which are, as it were, always readily to hand. This may be – though this is not the place to rehearse it properly – to say no more than that the concept and, what is more, the experience of difference lie deep at the heart of the SEN discourse.

And as researchers of SEN or disability, we give shape and weight to these dimensions of difference: we do not come innocent to a task or a situation of events; rather we wilfully situate those events not merely in the institutional meanings which our profession provides but also, and in the same moment, we constitute them as expressions of our selves. Inevitably, the traces of our own psychic and social history drive us. But because the institutional drive, shored up by finance, requires a public accountability we resort to method to clarify – though actually mostly obscure – our true involvement.

Now we might suppose that we slip method between us and those events, a soft of prophylactic will keep them distinct from us. But this is to misunderstand the nature, the *nature*, of method and its seamless identity with what it only apparently treats of. Science begins, says Michael Oakeshott (1933), '. . . only when the world of *things* opened to us by our sense and perceptions has been forgotten or set on one side'. The scientific way of seeing is identical with what it sees in its search for stability:

> The method and the matter of scientific knowledge are not two parties . . . they are inseparable aspects of a single whole . . . And the notion of the categories of scientific knowledge or the instruments of scientific measurement interposing themselves between the scientist and his [*sic*] object is a notion utterly foreign to the character of scientific experience. Without the categories and the method, there is no matter; without the instruments of measurement, nothing to measure.
>
> (ibid.)

And here it is: '"Nature" is the product not the datum of scientific thought' (ibid.).

The datum becomes, then, not the consequence of a way of seeing even, but that act itself (and as such must be intentionally opposed to the thing in itself). And in just this way are special educational needs produced by research.

This chapter is, I hope, no mere callow resistance against method. Nor, I believe, is it a romantic plea for the reconnection of behaviour and experience in a therapeutic. It is, if anything, a call for the reincorporation into method of the experiences and values which are set aside at the moment of, and as a condition of, the attachment of method. For me, this is a meaning of phenomenology.

For there are no instruments, no measures prior to the function of consciousness, and all instruments and measures depend for their very existence on the way they serve this function. Consciousness seeks objects – indeed is only knowable by the moment and way of its finding them. And the whole of this experience is primarily organized through an aesthetic.

Aesthetic attention to something is not a special or marginal case peculiar to (self-conscious) artists or their (sophisticated) audiences, but one which can be systematically developed by them only because it is the very foundation of intelligence. This is to say no more than that we attend primarily to objects in this way as a condition of our being in the world: we are here and embodied. But in the research experience we find ourselves occupied by a concern with the more patent and accountable forms of truth given with intellectual or material schemes. The 'research attitude', predicated on scientific principles, is methodologically opposed to art in its concern with explicitation.

THE MAN WITH THE BLUE GUITAR

At the beginning of this chapter I spoke of three writers whose work or words affected the organization of the ESRC study. There was a fourth, and a much more important fourth; this is Wallace Stevens, the American poet. Stevens' project as a poet is often described as epistemological; he is certainly occupied with the relation between 'reality' and 'the imagination'; and therefore with the relationship between individual things and classes of thing.

Stevens (1953) opens the long poem, 'The Man with the Blue Guitar', as follows:

> The man bent over his guitar,
> A shearsman of sorts. The day was green.
>
> They said, 'You have a blue guitar,
> You do not play things as they are.'
>
> The man replied, 'Things as they are
> Are changed upon the blue guitar.'

> And they said then, 'But play, you must,
> A tune beyond us, yet ourselves,
>
> A tune upon the blue guitar
> Of things exactly as they are.'

Among other things, this poem is about the relations between words and things, and about the capacity of art – including the careful use of language – to represent objects to us. Form, the poem says, makes things for us; even becomes the thing.

The project of art – the project of real expression – to represent 'things as they are' is surely no different for the researcher; and Stevens' guitarist acknowledges

> I cannot bring a world quite round,
> Although I patch it as I can.
>
> I sing a hero's head, large eye
> And bearded bronze, but not a man,
>
> Although I patch him as I can
> And reach through to him almost to man.

But the demand, the expectation of art (and here I should say the expectation of research also) is

> . . . to play man number one,
> To drive the dagger in his heart,
>
> To lay his brain upon the board
> And pick the acrid colours out,
>
> To nail his thought across the door,
> Its wings spread wide to rain and snow.

When I came to write of Nick, there was no method within the means of research would allow me to evoke him for a reader without violating, through reduction, the nervous complex of meanings which meeting and working with him provoked. Paul I had rendered this way, slipping the pieces of his life easily into boxes labelled with the cyphers and stuff of a social science. But Nick wouldn't go in.

I had thought to uncover Nick, and all the others, without realizing the absurdity of my own position: here was I presuming to tease apart the threads which made up the cultural patterns of personal and institutional life without so much as a glance at those which organized my own way of seeing; and without which those other lives would be invisible to me.

The realization of this absurdity led to much thought about method and methodology but chiefly it compelled me in a search for my own fossils. Of course it remains that there are many data waiting to be interpreted, and there remain probably many years' work of looking for a way sensitively and 'usefully' to report the experience and the 'findings' of the project. Having incorporated myself in this work, the task now is paradoxically one of how to make that self less intrusive.

I realize that this chapter raises rather than even starts to answer some profound questions, and that none of these is particularly novel; I also admit that I've ducked some important issues. And, after all, we inherit and live in a world organized by the 'method' which seems to be making me so confused at the moment. But my point, I think, is that we need always to look closely at the narratives which organize our experience and thus our identities, and not easily allow them to be subverted by the methods which, at the moment, we have to use.

Towards the end of 'The Man with the Blue Guitar', Stevens demands that we

> Throw away the lights, the definitions
> And say of what you see in the dark
>
> That it is this or that it is that
> But do not use the rotted names.

In part this chapter is a protest against 'the rotted names' which method provides and requires. Research demands that we make sense of the chaos of experience; what it has not yet allowed for is that this chaos is not a datum but is already organized by consciousness as the condition of insight, and the research finding is an identity arrested in a way of seeing, a way of putting it.

NOTES

1. Known operationally as COSEN (Constructions of Special Educational Needs), this project was funded by the ESRC between October 1989 and September 1991 as 'Teachers' Perspectives on Special Needs Policy and Practice,' award no. R000231910.

The main aim of the research was to document the experiences and effects of SEN and educational reform policies as they were expressed through local education authorities and schools, and realized in the daily lives of practitioners. This aim was realized through the following objectives:

- The description and evaluation of the structures and experiences of SEN developments within four 11–16 schools in each of four LEAs.
- The exploration in depth of the experiences, attitudes and professional orientations of some 30 staff within these schools, with particular reference to the 1981 and 1988 legislation.
- The relation of teacher conceptions of SEN to policy realization.
- The development of theoretical and methodological positions within an interactionist analysis of special education.

The LEAs and schools which participated were identified so as to provide a range of broadly different contexts and systems. There were three overlapping phases of data collection:

- Interviews with key policy framers in the LEAs and schools in order to build up a picture of the way in which SEN policy had developed and was constructed by those charged with developing and enacting policy.
- A questionnaire for all teachers in all participating schools, seeking information on their knowledge about and views on LEA, school and departmental policies, and about their experiences of those policies in action.
- Life-historical case studies undertaken with individual teachers to explore how their own life experiences, their beliefs, attitudes and values mediated the ways in which they interpret and develop policies.

2. I owe this thought, though not my version of it, to Neil Bolton.

REFERENCES

Bines, H. (1986) *Redefining Remedial Education*. Croom Helm, Beckenham.

Bogdan, R. and Biklen, S. (1982) *Qualitative Research for Education: An Introduction to Theory and Practice*. Allwyn & Bacon, Hemel Hempstead.

Bolton, N. (1981) 'Research and change'. Unpublished paper, University of Sheffield.

Burgess, R. (ed.) (1985) *Strategies of Educational Research: Qualitative Methods*. Falmer Press, Lewes.

Corrie, M. and Zaklukievicz, S. (1985) 'Qualitative research and case-study approaches: an introduction', in S. Hegarty and P. Evans (eds) *Research and Evaluation Methods in Special Education*. NFER-Nelson, Windsor.

Croll, P. and Moses, D. (1985) *One in Five: The Assessment and Incidence of Special Education Needs*. Routledge & Kegan Paul, London.

Eggleston, J. (1974) *Contemporary Research in the Sociology of Education*. Methuen, London.

Fulcher, G. (1989) *Disabling Policies? A Comparative Approach to Education Policy and Disability*. Falmer Press, Lewes.

Inglis, F. (1993) *Cultural Studies*. Basil Blackwell, Oxford.

Macdonald, I. (1981) 'Assessment: a social dimension', in L. Barton and S. Tomlinson (eds) *Special Education: Policy, Practices and Social Issues*. Harper & Row, London.

Oakeshott, M. (1993) *Experience and its Modes*. Cambridge University Press.

Pym, D. (1990) 'Post-paradigm enquiry', in J. Hassard and D. Pym (eds) *The Theory and Philosophy of Organization*. Routledge, London.

Schindele, R. (1985) 'Research methodology in special education: a framework approach to special problems and solutions', in S. Hegarty and P. Evans (eds) *Research and Evaluation Methods in Special Education*. NFER-Nelson, Windsor.

Stevens, W. (1953) *Selected Poems*. Faber & Faber, London.

Vulliamy, G. and Webb, R. (eds) (1992) *Teacher Research and Special Educational Needs*. David Fulton, London.

Walford, G. (1991) *Doing Educational Research*. Routledge, London.

Williams, R. (1965) *The Long Revolution*. Penguin, Harmondsworth.

Wilson, J. and Cowell, B. (1984) 'How should we define handicap?', *British Journal of Special Education*, Vol. 1, no. 2, pp. 33–5.

Wolf, R. and Tymitz, B. (1976) 'Ethnography and reading: matching inquiry mode to process', *Reading Research Quarterly*, September, pp. 38–56.

10

CONCLUSION: MANY URGENT VOICES

Len Barton and Peter Clough

As stories, the accounts collected in this book speak for themselves, and neither in our introduction nor here do we wish to provide a direct gloss on them. However, we believe that together they have a collective voice which we would like to reaffirm here; at the same time we would like – perhaps unusually – to make explicit our view of the contribution which we hope such work makes to the development of a sensitive and self-conscious research practice.

THE RESEARCHER AS CHANGE AGENT

All the accounts provided in this book are informed by a desire to see change take place at the material, institutional, political and attitudinal levels of society; barriers to participation, equity and human rights must be challenged and changed. This involves the researcher taking the voice of disabled people seriously, listening to them, exploring their lived experience in particular contexts. Getting beneath the surface to the personal feelings and experiences of participants is a significant aspect of this form of research. Thus it is sensitive, difficult and morally demanding.

If an essential aspect of what Oliver (1992) calls 'emancipatory research' is to identify and highlight how disabled people experience discrimination, and how they develop a positive identity, then it is vitally important that researchers, recognizing their limitations, endeavour to be more open and self-aware with regard to their own values, priorities and processes of interpretation. This, as the chapters in this book confirm, involves some radical changes to the way we as researchers plan, implement, interpret and disseminate our work and, significantly, the point and manner in which we involve the participants in such activities.

THE RESEARCHER AS CRITICAL FRIEND

It follows from the above that a particular interest of research viewed in this way is in capturing the 'voice' of disabled people and reasserting their right to speak and be represented. Historically, disabled people have been excluded, devalued and represented in largely passive and negative terms and this raises a series of ethical and moral tensions, dilemmas and anxieties for the researcher. Not only does this involve challenging in various ways and degrees those barriers to participation which disabled people constantly experience but also it raises some fundamental issues relating to the social relations of research production, particularly the power relations involved. As researchers we need to ask ourselves the following critical questions:

- What responsibilities arise from the privileges I have as a result of my social position?
- How can I use my knowledge and skills to challenge, for example, the forms of oppression disabled people experience?
- Does my writing and speaking reproduce a system of domination or challenge that system?

Research from this perspective is not about striving for some alleged disinterestedness but struggling to provide a form of engagement which is enabling to all concerned (Apple, 1986). Too much so-called academic research is largely irrelevant and of little benefit to the participants involved. Engaging with the issue of power is a key characteristic of high-quality research.

THE ACCOUNTABLE RESEARCHER?

Part of the endeavour of researchers becoming more self-aware includes addressing the question of 'accountability'. To whom is the researcher responsible and what form does this take? (Burgess, 1994). Tensions often arise over the network of relationships involved in any single research project and this entails competing definitions and interests. The expectations of the researcher, sponsor, subjects of study and the wider research community create, at different times, a series of complex and contradictory factors. These can influence how research questions are formulated, how research is implemented, how data is analysed and how the outcome is produced. This highlights issues concerning the purpose of our research and, as one disabled analyst advocates, researchers must seriously engage with such questions as follows:

• Who do I want this research to influence?
• Who do I want to be aware of this research?
• Who do I want to relate to this research?

(Morris, 1992, pp. 201–2)

But even with the best will and the most fastidious process, it is well to remember that intentions are no guarantee of outcomes; we must beware of an idealized, romantic view of both research and its impact. In rereading these chapters we were reminded not only that research is always partial and incomplete but also that the end-product is very vulnerable to a range of interpretations and uses. Once a document is in the public arena, the researcher loses control over how it is viewed and responded to by individuals or organizations. This raises the possibility that insights are used for purposes the researcher never intended and strongly disagrees with. This is a particularly serious issue in relation to those subjects of study who are oppressed and experience institutional discrimination. Researchers need to be 'culturally sensitive' therefore and learn to '. . . perceive risk factors from the perspective of the persons who will be affected, remembering that not everyone perceives things as the researcher would' (Sieber, 1993, p. 11).

THE RESEARCHER AS LEARNER

The authors in this collection have provided a series of personal reflections on their research which contribute to a growing body of literature that recognizes that the 'private troubles' of research need to become 'public issues'. By offering insights into the processes of their research the contributors have identified some of the benefits, contradictions and dilemmas with which they have had to engage, and from which they have learnt. They offer a form of story-telling, both their own and those of their respondents. This pursuit of making the subjective, as well as the taken-for-granted, public, requires the researchers to reflect on, evaluate and share, for example, the assumptions underlying their choice of methods and the ways in which they make sense of their findings.

Such accounts are important, not because they provide answers or a blue-print for the reader to follow, but because they raise difficult questions; the tales they offer demand extra effort on the reader's part, of aesthetic as well as a more traditionally critical attending. They evidence a sense of humility on the part of the authors, a humility at one with the perception of research as a personal quite as much as a professional learning process. Part of this learning involves challenging one's own existing values, priorities and expectations and, to be sure, working through an agenda of this nature is a very demanding emotional and intellectual activity; there are no short cuts or easy pathways: the process is problematic, risky and disturbing, and through their specific accounts the authors have provided some insight into these learning experiences which would otherwise have remained hidden.

THE RESEARCHER AS TEACHER

Our sense of audience with regard to the readership of this book illustrates one of the most central concerns of the book as a whole. How do we speak to an audience with such diverse backgrounds, experiences and interests? How can research find a voice – or voices – which can reach into the many different constructions of learning difficulty and disability which make up the broad community of special educational needs? How do we as researchers investigate the 'taken-for-granted' in a way which can both speak to those who 'take for granted' in terms they would recognize and at the same time challenge their orientation by holding up those terms to the light of radical questioning?

A partial answer to these questions, we feel, is to be found in the conception of the researcher not only as a learner but also as a *teacher*, and as such charged with finding the compelling voice; it is a conception of the researcher as persuader, as an explorer, as a raiser of consciousness, and not as a mere reporter. This is particularly applicable when research is concerned with those who are institutionally discriminated against and questions of social justice and equity are integral to the research act.

THE RESEARCHER AS SUBJECT

As Clough notes in this volume (p. 137), 'There have been many calls over the last 15 or so years for an empirical research in special education which would tell more persuasively of the matter and experience of learning difficulties and disabilities.' Schindele (1985), for example, cites as a major priority in respect of research objectives the exploration of meanings, of subjective definitions and complex relationships; citing Wolf and Tymitz (1976), he says (p. 42) that research must '. . . aim at understanding actualities, social realities and human perceptions'; of primary importance is the '. . . understanding [of] human behaviour from the subject's own frame of reference'.

What we hope this collection adds to that general project is a recognition that researchers, too, are subjects with their 'own frame(s) of reference', and that these frames reach beyond the idea of a neutral, value-free method/ology into the very lives of the researchers themselves. Put another way, we would say that the characteristically systematic nature and process of research in this area is not to be understood merely through the systems of a social science, but through the equally systematic, if more opaque, weave of personally lived values and experiences with which a researcher constructs, identifies and mediates his or her topic. So constituted, these points are as much expressions of researchers' lives as they are reports of the lives of their subjects. Research which sees the lives of researchers and subjects as oppositionally rather than continually related can only trivialize the real problems of research as mere problematics.

Of course all subjects – whether researchers or researched – act within an indispensably political arena; their acts variously realize policies as much as they are conditioned by them. But the framing, carrying out and reporting of research is an especially charged political act, from the identification of phenomena to the disposition of words which report them.

While we take this to be true of all research in the social sciences, we believe that it has a particular applicability in the case of SEN and disability issues in the inimical policy contexts of the 1990s.

REFERENCES

Apple, M. (1986) *Teachers and Texts: A Political Economy of Class and Gender Relations in Education.* Routledge & Kegan Paul, London.

Apple, M. (1993) 'What postmodernists forget: cultural capital and official knowledge', *Curriculum Studies*, Vol. 1, no. 3, pp. 301–16.

Burgess, R. G. (1994) 'Accountable to whom? Researchers and researched in education', in D. Scott (ed.) *Accountability and Control in Educational Settings.* Cassell, London.

Morris, J. (1992) Quoted in Jones, L. and Pullen, G. (1992) 'Cultural differences: deaf and hearing researchers working together', *Disability, Handicap and Society*, Vol. 7, no. 2, pp. 189–96 (special issue).

Oliver, M. (1992) 'Changing the social relations of research production', *Disability, Handicap and Society*, Vol. 7, no. 2, pp. 101–14.

Schindele, R. (1985) 'Research methodology in special education: a framework approach to special problems and solutions', in S. Hegarty and P. Evans (eds) *Research and Evaluation Methods in Special Education.* NFER-Nelson, Windsor.

Sieber, J. E. (1993) 'The ethics and politics of sensitive research', in C. Renzetti and R. Lee (eds) *Researching Sensitive Topics.* Sage, London.

Wolf, R. and Tymitz, B. (1976) 'Ethnography and reading: matching inquiry mode to process', *Reading Research Quarterly*, September, pp. 38–56.

INDEX